Mary Burritt
Christiansen
Poetry Series

MIRACLES OF SAINTED EARTH

MIRACLES OF SAINTED EARTH

VICTORIA EDWARDS TESTER

UNIVERSITY OF NEW MEXICO PRESS ▼ ALBUQUERQUE

Some of these poems have appeared in *Desert Exposure,*
Lunarosity, Poetry Wales, Red River Review,
and *The Drunken Boat.*

Library of Congress Cataloging-in-Publication Data

Tester, Victoria Edwards, 1964–
    Miracles of sainted earth / by Victoria Edwards Tester.— 1st ed.
        p.   cm. — (Mary Burritt Christiansen poetry series)
    ISBN 0-8263-2778-8 (alk. paper)
1. Southwestern States—Poetry. 2. Indians of North America—Poetry.
    I. Title. II. Series.
PS3620.E78 M67 2002
811'.6—dc21

                                2001005520

Design: Mina Yamashita

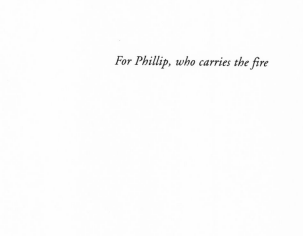

For Phillip, who carries the fire

Acknowledgments
Introduction

II YEAR OF LOVE AND DEATH

ACKNOWLEDGMENTS

I wish to thank my husband Phillip Tester who listened and listened—and smiled.

I wish to thank my mentor and friend, Patricia Lee Yongue, professor of English at the University of Houston. Without her steady warmth for poets, and the life of my soul, this book may not have come to be.

I am also grateful to: novelist Kathy Hepinstall and poet Laurie Newendorp, fiercest friends while we struggled in Houston; poet André de Korvin and his wife Marianne de Korvin; Elizabeth Gregory and Lois Zamora, professors of English at the University of Houston; and Rosellen Brown, Edward Hirsch and Cynthia Macdonald, my teachers at the Creative Writing Program there; Mary Burritt Christiansen (1923–1998) whose vision and generosity enabled this manuscript to become a real book, Dianne Edwards; Poetry Editor at the University of New Mexico Press, and Vincent Barrett Price, for their enthusiasm, kindness and patience in bringing my work into print.

I thank New Mexico artists Fawn Solimon Wyatt and Julian Perea, who nourished me with light; Virginia Gutierrez, Postmaster of the Heart; Virgie Allred and Niki Alsip, adventurous angels of Glenwood, New Mexico; and Alma Rosa and Wally Eavenson, for summer days in Mogollon.

I thank Jane Candia Coleman and Glenn Boyer, for their enduring wild and wonderful ways; Diane Freund, radiant in Bisbee; and Maria Vigil, who helps so much live, just outside Silver City.

xv

For this book I am indebted to my father Larry Edwards, for passing on his enduring love of the mountains and history of "New Mexico Territory," to my mother Beverly LaRock, for her respect for the struggles of our ancestors, to my sister in Oklahoma, photographer of spirits and tireless caretaker of the dead, and to my loving son Joseph who always inspires my bones.

—V. T.

Fort Craig, 1998

I got drunk on the smell of horses flying through creosote.

They were leaping through fifteen decades chased by a jealous cavalry

officer, dreaming of the broken glass I found near Washerwoman's Row.

Once it was a glass plate full of fresh strawberries held by an Irish

woman so lovely she could walk through bayonets.

It was out of her own blood she made the strawberries.

One for the night she spent rolling like a river under the horse

god of ecstasy. One for the hairy child who would not live. . . .

—Victoria Edwards Tester

I've always liked what W. H. Auden said of Marianne Moore—she had "an extraordinary gift for metaphorical comparisons which make the reader see what she has seen." I think the same could be said of Victoria Edwards Tester. I'm not trying to make an association, or a comparison, between Tester and Moore. But like Moore's poetry, Tester's refuses to be labeled. And her work reminds me of no one else's. It's not possible to call her a surrealist, a magic realist, an imagist, or a symbolist. She's not a regionalist. I can't say she bears the influence of Baudelaire, of Rilke, Lorca, Mistral, or of Kazantzakis either. Though, surely, they're part of a landscape she's at home in.

I find her work so emotionally compelling because she belongs to a community of poets heard more as voices from catacombs, tramp steamers, and long marches than as voices of orthodoxy, either tenured or coolly marginal. Latin America, occupied Celtic Europe, Welsh-Irish America, Apache and Comanche territory—she speaks from those long views and sorrows more than others I can think of. She speaks, too, as a woman who knows what it feels like to be censored and who defiantly resists self-censorship. The poems in this volume are free of predictability and marks of rehearsal, free of critical templates, liberated by attachments to real places almost nobody knows, and by a vatic intermingling of imagination and intuition.

Who is Victoria Edwards Tester? She's not eager to talk about herself. She'll go so far as to say she's Welsh-American, with Chiricahua Apache and Potawatomi ancestry. She lives with her husband on the fringes of what was once the old mining town of Santa Rita in southwest New Mexico. She also lives, she says, on forty acres in the Chiricahua mountains that border the Coronado wilderness. "We call that place Forever." She's thirty-seven, by my reckoning, a mother, with a Masters degree in creative writing and literature from the University of Houston, who abandoned the Ph.D. program there to move to New Mexico in 1994. But she's been connected to the "New Mexico Territory" all her life in the stories of her ancestors who lived and roamed here before the Civil War, her fierce grandfather who "had run wild" here in the 1930s, and by the love of her father for the land.

She's won her share of poetry prizes, including the Academy of American Poets Brazos Bookstore Prize and the Donald Barthelme Memorial Fellowship for Poetry. As for the academic life, however, she writes, "ideas are not good for poetry. Sometimes even the formal study of poetry is not good for poets. Because of this, my time in graduate school . . . was most often not a happy one. . . . I dreamed of being a professor, but never of doing those things that professors do. It reminded me of a story a Spaniard once told me about Lorca. A scholarly friend of the poet had answered Lorca's letter to him begging for advice about how to be a professional. 'Get a briefcase!' the scholarly friend had advised. My own 'briefcase' was going to be a doctorate. . . . Then, fortunately, a wonderful great arsenic lobster fell on my head. Broke the false form I'd imposed on my own life and shattered my briefcase. And carried me to New Mexico."

I don't know what or who that arsenic lobster was. But I do know Victoria Edward Tester's life has been filled with pilgrimages and strange journeys, including one when she worked as a journalist in 1992 for *Cairo* magazine of Cairo, Egypt. One harrowing experience is recorded in her poem "The Acorn" and described with chilling detail in her as yet unpublished memoirs. The story tells of rescuing her kidnapped son Joseph from his father in Peru. The poem reads in part:

> . . . *he finds an acorn*
> *my heart can't break. It is inside his chest.*
> *I place it there, the heart of a mountain lion.*
> *It goes to Peru, it defeats the death threats*
> *of his father, Hernán Patricio Pedro Bouroncle Gil*
> *and the Lima Senator Humberto Carranza,*
> *who said, on July 28, 1987, you will disappear.*
> *Its left claw tears a passport from the dome of heaven,*
> *it crosses the border into Bolivia.*
> *For my own heart I take the acorn. It is sixteen years old*
> *and it is a bitter aspirin.*

"Writing poetry, for me," Tester said in a recent correspondence from Santa Rita, "has become the willingness to be born again and again. This means into a world or a self or a shadow I do not know. . . . The ideal poem burrows its feet into the earth in enough places that you can follow it. If it is too abstract, it stares down at us from where it is circling above. We might respect it or try to guess at it, but we cannot love it or even shudder, the way we might when a red-tailed hawk flies so close that its wings' soft wind brushes our faces. . . . The poems I like best live their own lives and are marked by often invisible questions. The poems I like best are the ones that play. That have the wildness about them that flourishes when the human creature won't be leashed or caged."

What does she intend as a poet? When I asked, she answered: "a devout Attention, or the Listening Self. . . . But the self-creation of the Listening Self is mysterious. I don't know how it is done. . . . Always a word or a sound ahead of me, open, expectant, as if the creation of a poem has more to do with this listening than with the language that follows it. I believe I love the Listening Self more than the speaking self. I think the Listening Self is the most I know of God."

The poems in this collection listen to the past and to creatures, land, and ghosts who most people can't hear at all. Tester uses metaphor to its ultimate ability to reconcile and reconnect what rationally doesn't appear to belong together. In this case, she links her present life, the lives of her ancestors, the world beyond human nature, and the spirit of history and its unfolding in biography, with her spiritual love of the finite. The aesthetic excitement of her poems demonstrates as vividly as possible what we all know as a matter of common sense, but don't really pay deep attention to— that what happens in the present is a result of countless chances, choices, mishaps, aberrations, mysteries and tragedies of other lives interacting with landscape, climate, and historical predicament.

I've read this book three times, and I remain fascinated by the craftsmanship and visionary openness of her poems. None of them miss the mark. I have an affinity for some more than others, of course, but they all draw me in with the perfect pitch and intensity of their emotional and spiritual candor. I'm inspired by the generous, empathetic, and always energizing vitality of their metaphors. I remain intrigued by their seamless and beautiful joinery. And though they are rooted in specific places, her knowledge of where she is grows so intimate the poems would thrive in Paris as well as in Silver City. Her poems have that rare and astonishing Rilkeian inner knowledge of their subjects, that quality of getting inside historical figures and places, as well as animals and other natural forces, and listening to what they have to say.

"To go where I go in a poem," Tester wrote, "I follow a thread of sound. . . . The Listening Self goes first. It is my audience. It creates itself as I go along, always more powerful than the speaking self because anything can be listened to but not everything can be spoken."

Her faithful and welcoming attention, her open and eager listening fill Victoria Edwards Tester's poems with evidence of lives and places waiting for us to hear them.

—V. B. Price

ALBUQUERQUE, 2001

I

THE   BELOVED SPIRITS

I

Tonight I'll die in a dark room.
Filled with the history of yellow candles.
Blind to the fiery evidence of the winter solstice,
and the unhealed scars on God's oldest face.
To the dancing guests from heaven.
I'll go into the New Year,
accompanied only by the solitary gold
in the eye of the desert toad.
Who lived in my summer garden.

PINOS ALTOS

Under my skin, old churches, broken
roads to love and death.
At night I walk through the pioneer cemetery
with a man who wasn't raised by Jesuits,
but by the wind and the grasshoppers.
He holds my hand,
and suddenly I know he's a wolf.
He licks the lines of his free hand.
He's already seen how I'll abandon him,
and his delicate soul watches us
from behind the tree.

WINTER

Once I heard the earth introduce the dried sunflowers
to the birds, and saints to bones.
Once a car salesman was the yellow wolf
devouring my son's Peruvian father who'd jumped bail
to teach me a lesson.
Once when there was no winter wood,
I found the money buried in a tin can
beneath the snow of my own falling left breast.
My heart was a blue heron then.
It flew from the San Francisco to the hatchery and back
everyday. No one knew why, and my child learned
to draw the mourning dove, the egret and the tawny owl.
At supper the candle flames grew bigger than our pumpkins,
and our Seventh Day Adventist neighbors
sent us kindling for our stove:
in the blue heart of January in a house made of tin,
we threw Genesis and Ecclesiastes
and even the sweet Song of Solomon
into the fire.

CHIMAYÓ

It was after I saw the saints behind their iron grilles
and even the children weaving their tiny crosses
torn from the laughter of winter
jasmine into the saints' cages,
that I decided to leave my prison of grief.
When I opened my mouth an exquisite white spider
crawled into the world on her eight legs.
She walked across the static of the priest's voice
through the loudspeaker.
Blurring Spanish into a woven blanket to cover the bodies
of the lovers on the cement benches.
She built the skies of silken filaments so strong
not even the ghosts of one hundred cavalrymen
could pierce them.
I heard it clearly, for the first time,
that joy is my first duty.

CAVE CREEK CANYON, JANUARY 1998

I pray my son catching a trout in water so clear
it once blinded God. Who's wandered ever since through
these Chiricahua mountains, inside the holy trees
struck by lightning, behind the waterfalls
and beside the sleeping bears, who're resurrected
when the snow melts into creeks.
I pray my son now heading downstream. I pray him watched
from behind a trembling aspen.
I pray a boy with a shining fish in his hands.
What is good heals the wild eyes of the Holy One.
I pray my son turning towards You, who are
the sound of a deer out of hiding.
And seeing only the brilliance of the air that speaks of great runners.

HERO

Last night I dreamed a deer in the aisle of the church
watching over the little Mexican boy who was afraid to pray
for his feet to grow back.
They'd been pared away, like my hooves,
they'd left just enough to keep us standing.
We faced the altar, but the policeman guarding the way back
to the garden in the triptych blew his whistle
into the small heart we shared.
Then, Your sudden presence. A moment of laughter
in the mirror of justice. Which has the look of Villa's bright army,
or a multitude of rosebushes breaking through the cold
stone of the church floor.

THE BLUE BONES

Now the blue bones have asked me to follow.
They cross themselves, shining, a gate against bitterness.
They lay side by side. Pick us up, we're the blood of your lost twins.
They rub themselves together and make a fire
in the San Francisco mountains,
the fire that looks like a man's blue hips.
I ask why the blue bones burn
and they say because it is joy.
I ask why the blue bones burn
and they say because it is dark.

WEDDING SONG

There's an orchestra of juniper and piñon.
Finches and jays flying through those doors
in the sky my flute opens behind my ribs. They ache
where yesterday I began to stitch my shadow to yours.
Clever and industrious, piercing your blue fire under the blanket,
threading it to my burning snow.
This morning I leave my beautiful sleeping twin, who has
never known grief or jealousy, in our bed,
and come to the mountain alone. Where nothing runs away
from a shadow playing a love flute.
Tucking her dark wings deep into sunlight.

PHILLIP

When the cotton field flew away into a flock of eleven thousand
snow geese, I saw that I must never lose you.
I tore my blue dress and faced south,
hiding the lightning in my hands. Swallowing my curses,
the seven rusty embroidery needles in my veins.
Where I clawed your shadow, my two children walk
distrustful, holding hands in death.
What is your body, Phillip, but a wild patience that teaches
the grieving mare in my waist to run her own sadness.
I paint the two ashen crosses on my cheeks, the empty
white circle on my belly, and go back to bed.
When your truck leaves the mine at Tyrone I'll fly out
to meet you. Racing over the wet earth of your name.

THE WEAVERS

The weavers make our bed a meadow, they make us the bones
of Catholics and Protestants dead after their wars.

They wake us up laughing at the line they drew between us.
The draw us a circle around the earth that the bee flies,
they make us his teaspoon of honey.

They make your eyes a field of wild iris where horse thieves once hid,
they open the Scriptures to a page before Genesis.

They make us night, they spin our clothes off like stars.
They weave our waists to each other, they weave our first clothes.

They make us the first black and gold dawn, exploding with silence.

Everywhere, they make us gratitude, they grow it
wild out of the left sides of our bodies.

2

I am descended from Alice Gould's grandmother,
a Chiricahua woman paid for with seven horses
by a French-Potawatomi trapper.
From a narrow stairway of Puritan and Quaker
women called Grace and Thankful and Content.
Whether they were or not.
From Welsh and Scots women so clever and so poor
they made soup out of the stones where they kept their souls,
in order to avoid the taxes.

GRACE

When my fourteen greats grandmother Grace Livermore steps
from the boat to settle the Puritan colony of Watertown,
the rumors of the lost grant tremble to library dust
I read in my hand, and the legacy of the New World is blood.
I want to tear our page from history.
I want to say, Grace, stop, but I'm at her side as she disembarks.
Her shadow carries the light and misery of fourteen generations.
I can't turn back my twenty-one year old Uncle James, Civil War
Union sergeant of Engineering and Mechanicals. Turn back my beloved
sister, Judith, dragging her golden bellies through cemeteries
at the end of this second millenium to bring on her labors.
Turn back my own gentle shadow.
So I follow my young Grace across the plank,
and, my god, I hand her the shovel to dig her garden.

BIRTH

Before I betrayed you, sister, we were six horses, flying clouds
like shining porcelain bathtubs. We washed the flowing gowns
that smelled of gunpowder, and in our hooves we kept
the mute chapters of the history books.
That was before we were born, lured out of the wind
by a French-Potawatomi trapper and his Chiricahua bride.
Seduced by the curling vines of their names that escaped the old census.
I was the oldest, I made the bargain for both of us.
On our backs they traveled north to the rivers of Quebec.
To all those unlucky bottles of fire, to those traps full of ghosts.

OKLAHOMA

When I'm sick my throat closes. I burn with the joy
that has no end. I see you in the dark at Fort Sill,
walking through the old cemetery to bring on
your fourth labor. You're smoking
a passionflower cigarette and spying
on a stranger who's whispering stories to the red earth
of Geronimo's grave. Sister, you and I have wanted to be dead.
The way before we became women
we wanted to keep on being horses.
We already knew the ecstatic leap into silence.
How to go without riders. Freed from the blankets of our names.

FORT CRAIG, 1998

I got drunk on the smell of horses flying through creosote.
They were leaping through fifteen decades chased by a jealous cavalry
officer, dreaming of the broken glass I found near Washerwoman's Row.
Once it was a glass plate full of fresh strawberries held by an Irish
woman so lovely she could walk through bayonets.
It was out of her own blood she made the strawberries.
One for the night she spent rolling like a river under the horse
god of ecstasy. One for the hairy child who would not live.
One for the single word she learned in the horse language,
the sign for gift.
All the others were for duty. The plate was shattered
and she was dead even before she lit the lamp
and settled down to become these bones
I smell in the bright earth.

FIRST HUSBAND

It's true I poisoned you in the café off the narrow side
street in Lima, Peru.
It's true the sleeping tablets in the little box
would have turned a field of horses to bones in pine cradles.
You stirred their white powder into your coffee
like sugar, and after ten years I am still only sorry
for the horses. Paints who never existed.
Who would have died for you if they hadn't
woken up in the Chiricahua mountains.
Thundering out of my forehead like petroglyphs, like laughter.
Like those seven flames on the candelabra of the morning.

RESURRECTION

This April, twenty English sparrows come to rest on the piñon
just outside the window where the Kneeling Nun's frozen
in two hundred year old grief for her cavalry officer.
Who recovered and rode away with the ancient fork
I unearthed in the marsh,
the blood of dark children bleached from his shirt.
Remembering Mangus Creek, I counted sparrows
and found only nineteen. From the cottonwoods where I saw
the massacre, I knew the darkest would never arrive.
He died so that I could get out of bed thirteen decades later,
alive after so much grief. He's the weight of my falling
left breast. My palm filled with dirt.
My offering.

SPRING EQUINOX

This morning I walked out of hell, on a staircase
under the apple tree. Past the skeleton of the woman who died
throwing her body over her children. I sing to each blackened bone
but I can never bring her story back. They do say
her children live. That they push their grocery carts.
That they mate, sometimes like bulldozers,
sometimes like fields of wild iris.
That shining beer cans, like the molted feathers of the youngest angels,
fly out of their trucks at dawn.

SANTA RITA DEL COBRE, 1998

My good twin gets out of bed.
Her broom follows the muddy tracks of the stars
across the kitchen. I'm on my way home this morning
to a house that belongs to neither of us. There's no river,
only a porch that looks towards the Santa Rita Copper Mine.
I've been walking through the air above the open pit
where the town used to be,
looking for the rotten pieces of the barrels,
the shattered bowls of cornmeal,
the hoof prints in the old red powder.
The men I want are ghosts, they're the antelope
who survived the massacre in 1837.
All winter this mute woman has wanted my Irish husband
who's filled with the Baptist fury of God,
whose eyes drown the matchsticks in a bad woman's hands.
Take him, I told her, in February.
I'm going out to wander over the hot green
splendor of adultery.
The ghost of fire.
The red berry inside the warm tracks
that held their pure, bright bodies.

3

I went to find my Christ among tall grasses.
He was a deer pierced to an oak and forgotten.
The deer was a man, holy and burnt, like a snag.
Pulling the sword from his chest, licking it
clean with an oak leaf.
He opened the wet, red leaf like a book
and we sat down to learn
the hunter's language.

TRICKSTER

When they painted you china blue
and tied a red handkerchief around your neck
and sold you in every tourist shop
and even beside the road,
I knew it wasn't you.
When they blew away your liver
dropped your gold eyes into an antbed
cut off your balls for catfish
and strung you up on a roadsign off the highway,
I smiled because I knew that it was you, that
we had met.

THEY PLAN COYOTE'S DEBUT

It's springtime in the leg bone of the coyote.

They're revamping the old musicals and getting ready to throw popcorn.
They're dancing the bone on a velvet chair
and giving him standing ovations.

They're setting a table for him, all Depression glass and Nambé.

They're escorting him up to Santa Fe to show him in the galleries.
They're hauling him back to Silver City. If he's from California
they'll sell him a new mobile home.
They're steering him away from the stubble of the ranches,
and pointing out the fattest cows in the National Forest.

They've planned his debut in the hardest New Mexico roles:
As anybody's son cruising the Sonic killed in a driveby shooting.
As Última, in her grandson Rudolfo's white suit, speaking
to a crowd of welfare mothers.
As an anonymous woman from Sonora who drowns swimming
the Rio Grande, but nevertheless manages to speak to reporters.

They've scheduled an appearance in Truth or Consequences
in order to revive the old gameshow.

In Deming they want him to work picking chile.
He's been elected by the union to help save the Kneeling Nun.
The bosses have ordered him back to the casinos.
He's been hired as a tourist guide to the fascinating life of the Pueblos.
Mothers Against Drunk Drivers has asked him to pose
as a white cross on Highway 180.

The border patrol has threatened to apprehend and rape him
if he goes around without his papers.

The Catholics have suggested that he leap up onto the cross.
The Baptists are begging him to be born again.
The Seventh Day Adventists have volunteered to wash his tired feet.

The Pueblos just want him to bow out politely and come home.

He may end up working at a convenience store, selling Skoll.
He may live with his half-sister's daughter in an old school bus.
He may get drunk and hit seven horses while hauling three stolen pianos
in his uncle's truck, and do time in jail.

Or his ghost may gnaw off the leg he's caught in the rusted trap
I found in the San Francisco river, and leave us
just this bone.

APRIL

When I heard an old woman whistle through the bones
of April to find the sun, I went back to bed.
I'm too cold to wrestle with the resurrected wild iris
or ride out to welcome my sisters the sand-hill cranes
who have been back from the dead for a month.
I'm too weak to lift the coffeepot
or lay my hand in the cold ashes of the wood stove.
Where my laughing twin says if you're not fast
you'll meet the slow speaking ghost
who smokes Lucky Strikes.
Only half-ghost, he's a horse below the waist.
All through spring he jumps the corrals
of those housewives who live without the sweet
holy water of a baby's loud screams.

COFFEE KLATCH

Sister, this morning you're planting horsetail
for the six strong pairs of kidneys
the devil's tricked into your hands,
and laughing like a golden dog
because you're thinking of slapping a strong love tea
on your husband. Who looks like Teddy Roosevelt
in those little round glasses.
He's told you he's hairy enough for two, that he thinks of nothing
except spreading your thighs from dawn to dawn,
but you're not convinced. You say the tea will make him
an animal, the elk who comes to you in your dreams like a king.
Or it will kill him.
And you're willing to take your chances.

Yesterday I stole my blue willow plate back
from the old church in Mogollon
because I didn't want the Virgin
to make that cavalry officer turned car salesman
love me after all.
It would be bad luck to leave it there.
After all, I'd met you, the living half-deaf twenty-eight greats
grandson of Saint Francis.
Who they say was a real musician and carouser
until the tragic day the Holy decided to haunt him
in a voice like wild mint blowing on the sides
of a clean creek. Four hundred years later they boxed
that voice and sailed it here, to New Mexico,
to harass the bodies and souls of the plants and animals,
men and women. If anyone understands the pickle
of lust, it's Saint Francis.
So I didn't lower my eyes when I carried
my blue willow plate out of the church
they named for him. The empty clothes hanger
that wired the door shut was the horse
shape of your naked shoulders
and hips, riding me tonight, if you were willing.
Then the rickety wooden porch where I crossed
my fingers the Holy would keep His mouth shut.
For that silence, I thank the open yucca pods
I left on the altar. All those tiny black yucca seeds,
like the thousand pieces of the night sky broken
only by its lucky stars.

I'm throwing rocks at your window, inspired by the antique
teapot carved with thistles and dandelions. The silver's
rubbed off and the teapot's the color of the dust
of a big breasted woman who never stepped out of the blue
circle of her dress into the hell of a man she loved.
He lived in a ruin that history would patch
with his old medical texts on venereal disease,
and yellowed newspapers from the eve
of World War II. She was scarred from the Arizona brothels
and kept her thighs locked like a pie pantry
in a cool mine shaft.
He was an Eastern doctor but he couldn't see the flu epidemic
coming through the ocean of pines he never spoke to,
like a majestic mother-in-law
who wouldn't answer him in English, anyway.
They had to put away their milk and their rage,
their heat and their forgiveness
into quickly built pine boxes.
They had to tear the flesh from their longing,
the wind from their old nursery rhymes.
They had to become the bear grass
ripping through the cemetery on the road above Mogollon.
Come and sit with me. I don't want to be this owl. My head
turning around backwards, looking alone into another century.

STATE ROAD 117

Let's mate in this malpais, where it's difficult to walk, even.
You pull the clouds over me like torn white flags,
so I won't burn to ashes in the sun.
I'll open my legs wide for the flash of your river,
so you won't be lost to the juniper and the rabbit brush.
That's how we'll save ourselves, my love.
That's how I'll save us, through telling all these lies.
Sometimes I lie so much you fall asleep.
Then I get so beautiful the wind wants me
for his own wife.
The curious bones of his spying deer
chime in the thorns around us.

I invent a brother in the solitude of this valley,
where my husband is silent too.

My brother's ignorant, he's a vision of an angel inside Spanish armor.

He's a miracle boy who stands up fully grown in a field in County Cork
during the Irish potato famine.

He's blind as Saint George standing on a dead dragon.

The vasectomy won't be reversed, there'll be no new baby.
So I swing my brother on my hip, the schoolhouse of the world.

This is lust and this is love and this is hate.
This is how to dig the tangled roots of stars and wonder
what that sound was years ago.

This is the little town
of Paradise they made as a refuge for the cutthroats
who were run out of Tombstone. The world is broken,
I tell my brother. You will never be born, or understand evil,
which is a vital organ of our souls.

My brother's an angel who spends his one day on this earth on Highway 80,
trailing the echoes of God.
Those echoes, the roads we must walk
that go east and west and north and south at once.

Those tiny crosses that lead through the heart
of this mesquite.

They're not always smoke.
Sometimes they're holy idiots, who step out
washed and bleached, like new clothes.
They're like us, only happier, and they can't be harmed.
They already carry our ashes. They laugh past the carnival of apple blossoms
dead on the branches in Chimayó.
They suck oranges as if they were the fallen domes of heaven.
They follow the ten Christs who wind through the heart
of the mountain lion.
They read the scraps of rusted tin the Holy tears
like postcards from the roof of the chapel.
They love what's fallen, what's rebuilt.
Above all, they honor dogs. Above all, they love devotion.
But the great ones aren't meek about it.
They love devotion the way the damned
loved the fiercest angels. The way they opened their arms
to those great ones
who rained fire, and burned their hearts down
to this holy ground.

4

GIFT

Not even the small deer's antler
I've hidden under our mattress
can curve the straight road of this dream:
You carried the soft bread that I baked for you
tucked under your arm, even to the charred
doors of heaven.

Mother of God, let's stay alone in this world.
Let's go unnoticed, twin spikes of wild iris.
Or two empty milk cartons on the soft shoulder of the highway.
Anything but follow them to heaven.
Anything but follow the renowned architects' shining blueprints
for our souls in the afterworld.
I don't ever want to leave this fallen place they have betrayed.
After this open roof over pines and bears, after the true mists
of the Mogollon mountains,
I never want to see the face of God.

It might be ridiculous that the sweet Mother of God could love us.
Or answer a prayer like that, when she does nothing
except appear sometimes when the wind blows
the horse brush in Skeleton Canyon,
holding a cactus wren in her thin brown hands.
They say if a river ever flowed here at the foot of the Peloncillos,
it's been dead for a century.
There's no use looking through old campaign maps, or
the torn diaries of cavalry officers, or the delicate letters
their wives sent back East, like pioneer tears
for fringe on those Tiffany lamps.
Because you will never resurrect a river
from the dust of a library,
and Cochise County is a cemetery of rivers.
There are days I want to drink glass after glass of this sand.
I want to drink to the bottom of this mystery.
Down to all of the love, all of the death.
Down to the day the Mother of God reappears
in a flowing dress that is blue and green and sewn
with small gold threads.
It's ridiculous, and maybe it's wrong,
but when she lays down under the thighs of the young
cottonwood, the gold threads leap off.
They're river otters and cattails and trout.
And that's how she gives herself back to us.
Mine's a joy that makes no sense.

THE ACORN

My son Joseph without a shirt is hanging
his work jeans from the clothesline.
If only the neighbor to the west didn't collect bones.
If his tin house wasn't set in a nest of bones
of animals he shot running from his yard.
If he hadn't strung that pit bull corpse to rot.
If he were at the Hanover Bar, staring at the fires I've set
in the bottom of his whisky glass.
Because for the past four Sundays my son's body's been
long and graceful. He eats the tall grasses I've abandoned
to the yard. From the west he's in clear view of our neighbor,
his bare chest the brown of a deer. When he turns
to smile at me where I stand in the doorway
because he finds an acorn
my heart can't break. It is inside his chest.
I place it there, the heart of a mountain lion.
It goes to Peru, it defeats the death threats
of his father, Hernán Patricio Pedro Bouroncle Gil
and the Lima Senator Humberto Carranza,
who said, on July 28, 1987, *you will disappear.*
Its left claw tears a passport from the dome of heaven,
it crosses the border into Bolivia.
For my own heart I take the acorn. It is sixteen years old
and it is a bitter aspirin.

I dream that Ben Lily, tough mountain man
who killed five hundred mountain lions,
is a rabbit. God has made him afraid.
His small red eyes watch us from the darkness
of the San Francisco mountains.
I talk to my dog and to my husband who was raised in the Burros
and they don't listen when I cry over those lions
anyway. I say, that's only the ghost
of Ben Lily, mountain lion turned inside out to the bones
of a cottontail, all shivering.
Lick one of these junipers before you throw it
in the fire, and you'll smell the pure salt of his wife,
who said, one more hunting trip, you don't come back.
They say that Lily took his gun and closed the door so soft
behind him that woman's heart fell straight to the bottom
of her barrel of cornmeal. And his children lined up to say good-bye,
like bits of floating salt pork, in the yard.
After Mrs. Lily fished out her heart and set it
back beneath her ribs to do the washing, she told those children:
Don't cry so loud. Your father's gone away to punish
those loud lions. He's jealous he's only a rabbit.
Because rabbits make the softest tears of all.

There's a darkness at your shoulders
that was here even before the mountain mahogany.

Before this cap rock and this old wagon road from Georgetown
that scratched its way to the top of the mountain.

Before the valley below began to blaze and fade
with cattle and the yellow stars of cottonwood and death.

This darkness doesn't offer any wisdom.
It doesn't reprimand, and it has never punished anyone.
This darkness only waits.
It's like broad daylight that way.
It's like everything except Revelations.

You can pray yourself sick, and it will never be the left hand of God,
or a furious angel with a shining trumpet.

It will never be anything except a darkness at your shoulders
that was here even before the mountain mahogany.

THE BONES OF FATHER GERÓNIMO

Twelve years later, October, on the way to Bernardo, I remember
how that gypsy's curse chased me into the taxi in Lima, Peru.
Everything under the sky begins to stink.
I become a perpetual stranger.
I forget Spanish, and what's worse, the stinking immigrant
salt cedar has turned to gold along the river.
Then the bones of Father Gerónimo begin to stink,
all the way from Santa Fe, where they were called back
after four hundred years by the once fragrant Archbishop.
That Father Gerónimo, sweet Franciscan who drank Pueblo
urine in the shade of yellow flowering horsebrush
until they felt pity and took him in at Quarai.
But because I've been cursed, because now I'm a stranger
and everything stinks, I can't forgive
such gentleness, on either side.

TO MY HUSBAND

You throw me to the wolves, but they are kind.
They set a table for me, blazing with candles and forks.
They tell you I'm not Christian, that I'm no longer
a Christian, and they make no apology that my brown eyes
of a deer don't match my heart. They say they kept the deer's heart
from me, in a box they made of Santa Rita snow and piñon.
They gave me one of their own hearts they found on fire.
One they snatched from the flames while the starving hunter
who looked just like you was singing to the coldest stars.

ROTTEN OAK

Dawn, I walked over Santa Rita snow to find that good
piece of rotten oak for the wood stove.
It was a dangerous light.

That time when the light of the earth
hasn't decided whether it will be spirit or human
when it passes over us. I stood there in my sandals,

I took my chances as it crossed. It felt like the warm shadow of a hawk.
It felt like giving up.

This time it was lifting me out of the cold.
The oak got light. Half of it followed the hawk
up, because its bitter acorns fell a long time ago.

The other half was still heavy and dark with snow,
so I stayed on this earth
and carried it back to the stove.

Because that's what love is.
Carrying the ghosts of fire in the wreaths of our arms.

And going home and going home and going home.

They take us back in October.
They take us to the unmarked grave
in Okemos. They give us the old photograph,
our great great grandparents, 1910.
They met in Quebec.
Her face is full and deep with Indian silence.
His Welsh shoulders are narrow as his old violin.
They say she had a rare laughter that turned acorns to honey,
and she liked to drink a whisky that freed a river
otter live from a rusted trap.
They say he was a farmer who never tasted anything but water,
but he opened the doors to heaven on his fiddle
and it looked just like a barn dance.
We were told the secrets of their dying, and if you are gentle, I'll tell you
her liver will fail, and he will break his thigh
and not let his daughter-in-law Belle call a doctor.
They looked at us with the black and white look love
has when it is fighting history.
Eighty-nine years later their grandson, our Great Uncle Free
opens the bottle of wine
he made from the fruit of the Michigan elderberry.
He sets four glasses of wine, and one of water, on the table.
We drink with them so they can see into the fires
of our hearts, those fires that are purple and black
like the elderberry. The sweet fires facing east and west,
and those that grow on the north and south
and always have a bitter taste.
Sister, they teach us to be glad we are here,
and to hurt, and not to hurt.
They teach us that to love is to drink fire, and to burn
like the beloved spirits in an old photograph.

Over the snow and the piñon, no hawk answered us.
Instead, the coyotes, who also belong to no one.
Husband, last summer when we were children we said their barks
meant death. We said those dogs were bells ringing
our last hour, so we ran laughing until our lungs crashed like high
branches in the cold. We ran all the way to Christmas,
which is the first hour of the earth.
Now we are here, in the hour of fire
where the forest begins to move over
our hearts, blazing a new year.

DECEMBER

Phillip, gentle lover of horses,
you bring the Christmas dawn.
You are the sun
in a letter from God.
My ravens fly out of the oaks,
parting the red wax seal
of this pure envelope.
The year I spent asleep, I was your black horse,
and the fields
you crossed at midnight, over all the dead.
I was your true wife,
the two women who go with you,
and our laughter resurrected
the tall grasses of this earth.

II

YEAR OF LOVE AND DEATH

I

I'm a lovely box of hummingbird dust.

My hips have fallen
into bones, nectar, and two teaspoons
of holy New Mexico dirt.

This may be my last spring. The mattress
of our Civil War bed
is wearing so thin we feel the dark ground
under this mining shack
beneath us now.

My spine may not make it back.
For two weeks now it's been ironed against
the sweet broken hearts of mice,
skunks and javelinas.

When I go outside, my shoulders slope
towards last October's mullein,
blazing like my thirty-five birthday
candles in the yard.

My bottom is dragging like antique silver
in an old flour sack.

My feet point east and west now,
rather than straight from the splintered porch
towards the Kneeling Nun.

I don't believe her legend anymore.
They lied when they said love for a man's
freshly bathed body
turned a religious woman to stone.

It's virtue that turns to stone.
Love falls apart so much it's more like dying.
Not at all like a monument.
After a while you can't tell it from the earth.

BLESSING

From the porch this morning it was the first blue
bird on the juniper.

So bright the Kneeling Nun on the mountain
was startled into a woman gathering verbena
to wash her breasts in their sweet water.

I knew right then if a woman who died of a grief
torn between God and a cavalryman

could walk around naked and happy,
after being only a virtuous stone for two centuries, then

I wasn't afraid anymore of Phillip's old Harley,
glowing bright orange not twelve feet from me,
next to the flowering pear.

I decided to let the snapdragons die too
since they couldn't go a day without water.

I decided there was nothing we needed
from the damned store today, or this year.

Nothing we couldn't find
somewhere in the back of the cupboards
or in some weed growing in our dirt.

There, I saw my husband
standing in candlelight.

The dust of the Tyrone mine was on his face.
He was asking me for nothing, except to stand there
smiling at me through the dust
on his face. I saw it was May 1st.

Time to place his hands on the strings
between my breasts,
that sound better than his Martin guitar, even.

Then that bluebird flew up, dropping the air like a blue
handkerchief over my head.
It was a blessing from Marie,
my three greats grandmother who is in heaven.

Who watches us sometimes through those birds
who are as sky blue as her body.

Last November you painted the rusted iron bones
of the bed frame we hauled from old
Georgetown bright red.

That blazing frame lay against the juniper all winter,
like firethorn winding towards this year's spring
equinox. I was in Oklahoma then,

carrying a gallon of Great Uncle Free's
homemade wine
through the Indian cemetery.

With a sister who was laughing and showing me the Queen of Hearts
hid up her denim sleeve.

It had to do with blowing into the dust
of four white horses, and running them home for a husband
to feed while he was watching the static
of stranger women's breasts on TV.

And how to smoke a passionflower cigarette without choking
and offer it and prayers to those who were laying
under the broken lilacs.

Fast, before the mosquitoes took all your blood back
to the lake
and came back as thousands of locusts
with their own orchestras.

The Bible says we do not know the Hour or the Day.

But for love, I will always return,
even after that.
Even from Oklahoma.
Even from the cemeteries.

To you, my love in New Mexico,
with that color of ochre and hope on your hands.

OCOTILLO

The ocotillo leads to the sky, a lot like love.
It's a terrible desert ladder no fool wants
to climb.

The blood red flowers that wave at enemies
from its six peaks make a tea

sweet enough for calling back the ghosts
of one hundred lost hummingbirds.

So be it, I said, even if it's unlucky and hardly
ever done. And yesterday I whistled
like a boiling kettle
and bent a long, thorned branch

towards the direction of my 1924 gas stove.

Right then my angry Phillip leaned
my way, after so many hot days had turned us
to arguing shadows.

I made a tea that turned us
both to sunlight. We smiled so hard
you could not see us.

We filled everything.
Every arroyo. The cold soul of the snake
under every rock.

With the softness of the great and harmless God
who sings over this Chiricahua earth.

THE WOLVES

My two husbands barefoot on the porch.
One with a razor in his left hand,
a glass of water in his right.

The wind, howling like wolves in a circle
around the house.

They've come for what's theirs.
The hairs from the body of a man
who's walked one hundred
and fifty-two years past the Irish famine.

With the help of a grandfather
who crossed the Atlantic to distill whisky,
become a teamster.
Another who walked out of the forests of Michigan
pushing a vegetable cart.
Hid his Indian like Canadian pennies
in a jar in his chest, sugar maple leaves gone
to copper and grease.

Indian man who dangled a goose head
from his mouth like a necklace.
Maybe he did it to get rid of company.

Story of drawing a kiss
from another man's fine wife with the luck
of the Irish,
like getting water from an abandoned well
that tasted like a loving woman.

The wolves come for their right,
like they do, to the luckiest.
They sharpen the razor
and they cloud the water.
They take the wild Irish hairs
and give us back dust devils,
agaves, spring oak leaves.

I hold the antique mirror
against my heart so one husband
can see the other,
and they claim they shave for two loves
of the same wife.

I hold the mirror so the wolves
can see we have obeyed
the springtime's lovely justice.

My husband on the guitar is playing the grief off the doves' eggs.
He's playing the eggs in twos, in fours.

He's playing the newborn doves,
who smell of cinnamon and milk and sighing.

I saw exactly what would happen if we laid down on that bed
when it was time to work.

Pretending we were going to take a nap.
We can't even fool ourselves.
Let alone the dog. Let alone the sun
descending on bright Martin strings to the west,
behind the rose cliffs.

I'm undone by love, and he's filling the house with gentle birds
waking from their nests on the ground.

And they're telling us how the eternal hunger and peace
break into music again and again, among a few dried grasses.

THE MULBERRY

The mulberry you never brought for my birthday
is rhyming in a circle around us now.

It's carved itself into bows in the spring wind.
Bows that kill deer and skunk, and even
shoot through the one humble joy of mice
and the arrogant joys of green hummingbirds.

The gray rabbit in my heart is pierced
and falls dead too. I wash him like a shirt
and iron him straight. I melt him into silver
and set the table.
Two knives, two soldiers hiding in the woods.

Ever since the little carved grouse fell
from the wind hole of the flute and got lost
on our walk over the side of the mountain,
our love has been broken.
And now for my birthday, not even
a grouse made of juniper.
Not even the dew on the juniper berries.

I don't want to listen to this morning's Baptist
sermon on marriage.

The ten thousand white heron of my body
visit you on their ways
back to dawn.

On that morning the drawling minister
Jesse Lyles
and our beloved radio
will be one more small light sparkling
on a trout in Cave Creek.

I have nothing against goodness,
or even the law of Moses.
They may be the dusk's earliest ten stars.

But it's because I believe in the return of the rivers
that I stand over supper
in this kitchen in Santa Rita
until my hips turn to marsh
and turtles sing in my legs.

That I lay with you in the evening
and ask you to love
and witness a calling that rises and whirls
around wetness.
My body's ten thousand trumpets.

That I'm asking you to forget our marriage
and our civil duties
and be my true husband.

That crazy blue-eyed Irish promise
of the resurrection of the marsh at San Simon.

2

When the small brown hill
blindfolds Cochise like a fort,
turn south on Highway 80.

Walk through the needles
of the cholla,
the ocotillo, the mesquite.

Give anything you've got
for a drink at the dead
San Simon marsh
where water has not run for a century.

Bargain anyway,
and spit out of kindness
for the ghosts of the otter.

Sister, when you climb out
of the eaten valley,
when you climb to my house
on the side of the mountain,
I can't hold you.

For love, they've given me a bramble.

They've taken my heart
and given me the blackbird's wings.

ELK

I deceived my husband with the elk who glides
behind juniper and oak.

When an Irishman's in the forest,
he follows his wife north with the moss,

trails her clothes thrown off like rotten leaves.

True, I died when he found me.

But not before I lost the sun, I lost the tall grasses,
and the golden ring behind my ribs fell
to my ankles and I kicked it off.
I stood on my back hooves so I could reach the juniper berries.
Instead I reached fragrant pieces of the moon on a twig
that tasted like light.

Instead, I found my tongue licking a brown calf
to her knees. She was my soul,
and she hardly knew how to walk

before she ran for joy.

HAWK

That hawk was riding a tumbleweed, blown
seventy feet into the air. Looked like for the fun of it.
Whoever thought of that.

Joy in riding a fragile world of brittle skeleton
you know you'll lose at the first rain
to a rusted fence or the bottom of an arroyo.

But there hasn't been so little rain in forty years.

The neighbor says the oaks are going to die,
and don't worry, even if the rainy season comes,
these mountains are a lightning rod.

I turn away. They say she sleeps with her father.
They say they run bulldozers over the ancient burials, hoping to leave
at least one small bowl unbroken.

They say it's easier to be an oak struck by lightning.
That a tall burned snag is another
of God's holy fingers.

ROAD

It's been a hard evening.
The sheriff drove away with our signed witness statement.
Our neighbor's suing because we made tracks on his land
and drove over some rabbitbrush.

I'm wondering if he's going to paint our names
on the plywood cemetery he's erected
for his enemies going south on Highway 80 towards Douglas.

And still the mother of the spotted fawn has not returned
from where she ran when our dog dragged what we thought was a rabbit
screaming from the dead agave.

It's unharmed where I laid it down against the earth
after I held it like it was my own. Bones
I was keeping from the coyotes.

One of these days we're going to barbecue
with the sheriff and his wife
because she plays acoustic guitar like a blue silk angel,
or a rope of rain in May I'd like to hang myself on.

I am looking at the long line of the Peloncillos
and have no where to walk, except Paradise.

I'm a deer without milk.
I'm a judge without a law.

On the road to Paradise, the raven takes
my heart so I can laugh at the way it calls
from that dead oak.

FAWN

It's raining on the fawn and washing our scent away,
or so we hope.

I'm worried she'll drown and want to cover her with dead agave,
but you say that's against good judgment.

I hear the coyotes eating their own tails to the South.

We leave her to die if her mother doesn't return
from the veil
of oaks higher on the mountain.

Midnight I am wailing to the sound of flesh torn from bone,
the crucifixion of an innocence I held in my arms.

RUBEN GONZALES

They say you're going to die
Ruben Gonzales

in two weeks when the monsoons
thicken into rainbows
and fall like foals in the valley.

They say you'll stand with liver cancer
and dance with your broom named Elizabeth

under the earth
to a radio no one in New Mexico has heard.

Because you go, the green lizard
will find his wedding ring

and show it off to everyone who can see
into gold, into shadows.

Ruben, may the door in the mountain open,
may you enter like the honeybee
who met Cortés
and sailed east to live on for another five centuries.

May your right hand hold a sun
you've tricked into a red chile.

Those of us who stay behind
call your left hand Montezuma,
we call it Hummingbird,

call it Love, and kiss it
as it goes.

BY LAMPLIGHT

My husband's hands on the strings
of his guitar while the mountain lion

licks the deer's liver and I tremble at the October
falling against a single oil lamp.

We used to speak to each other,
each sentence marked with twelve blessing
questions like the trill of quail in shadows.

When we finished all the speaking, we were oaks.

We had yes and we had no.

Harder than these pale rose cliffs. Harder than love,
and the wind that carves the rose cliffs.
Just as ordained. Just as alone.

THE HISTORIES

When we sleep the deer return
for their bones.

They drink through the oak leaves
floating on the waterhole.

They turn towards the naked hearts
we hide behind storm windows.

They trample us like thunder. Like whisky, and the histories
blowing through the verbena at dawn.

Midnight when I piss in the blue enamel pot,
I know it is useless, they're not deer at all.

They're an army riding towards us,
on the backs of the wrong horses,
in the wrong winds.

And they will never go back beneath the oaks
until we have given them
our deep tears for their souls,

and all we have ever seen of this earth's
butterflies gathering
pollen, for their bones.

3

GOOSE HEAD

I dream your two greats granny Angelique Prairie
dipping turtle soup
with a wooden spoon.

They say her Indian name was White Deer
and she ran like a pattern of lightning
through Toledo, Erie
and Devil's Lake, for the love of a trader
named Joseph Laberdie.

It was next to the River Raisin.
Bet you can't catch your fancy French husband
and stick this goose head in his mouth.

Before White Deer dropped her ladle, Joseph
began running towards his half a chance, his knees bending
with the hard pride of the turtles
his wife had stewed for twenty years.

There was so much laughter in the forest when White Deer
zigzagged to his side and tripped him
he thanked God for the blood
where his head hit that log.

He thanked Jesus for the sweetness of losing
to a woman no other man could
catch, and he parted his teeth
for that goose head.
Carried it, triumphant, back to camp.

On Halloween of 1873, I, Mollie Metcalfe,
went by wagon to the ranch where my father

James lived in a one-room cabin. Walls and floor were rock,
the roof was earth. Another room on the east side
and a jacal on the north for the horses
whose hard hooves and breath were our nighttime
lullaby. We chained the horses against the Apache

because we didn't know their superstition,
their feeling for the old burial ground.
They never bothered us, but we watched
our step. My father pushed his vegetable cart
in Silver City, but our first winter on the Mangus
was hard as a bush without berries. We had no
milk or butter. Flour, sugar, lard and coffee cost
more than we had. We had wild ducks and sacks of dried
buffalo meat that made a good hash. We had corn
and squash raised by water from what we called the Montezuma dam

the Indians used before us. We had no church,
no school, no neighbors, but Dave Evan's team of oxen
brought our mail. Indian attacks and elections
were our excitement. The winters were not near
as bad as Missouri's. My mother and her stepmother scraped

corn shucks for cigarette papers that sold in Silver City.
Heaven came down in wild grapes, cherries, mulberries,
wild currants and the little native walnuts.
We made our furniture. We had one pair of shoes
and one dress, every three years.

There was a celebration I could not attend
in calico. We fed the soldier's horses. Five cents
per pound for gamma hay, six cents for corn. My father
brought the one or two officers back from camp
for a ranch supper. Sixty years later I can see

those uniformed men standing under our willow dirt
roof, bowing solemn as jackknives to my sweet-faced
mother. We built a four-room house of thick adobe
in the summer of '75, but for six more years it had no
shingles. I taught myself to sleep with pans on my bed
and in the morning I poured that water
on my mother's small apple tree.
I am glad to help you remember these old times,
and if I can do anything else along these lines,
I will always be ready,
as long as I am alive. Mollie Metcalfe, Palo Alto, California, 1933.

On December 22, 1882, an old newspaper
reports a demented woman was sent from Georgetown
to the Grant County Jail.

Sheriff Whitehill is at a loss,
poor creature, New Mexico law makes
no provision for paupers or the insane.

Her name, where she was born, or if she had a sister
who loved flowering dogwood branches
are secrets lost among the broken colored glass,
the pioneer tears
I've gathered among fallen mining shacks.

I wonder if it was the brothel.
If it was one man, or one hundred.

If it was a small crack in a treasured Tiffany lamp
that split her like kindling.

Or the disease of a season,
not too far from midnight singing to the mountain
mahogany, maybe taking a small one for a child
to forget the one in the cemetery.

I wonder if she went to California, on
one of those wagonloads of the insane.

Someday I'd like to make a stained glass window
from these sharp tears I've stolen
from the earth.
But it would never go inside a church.

It would hang against the sky,
in memory of everyone who broke.

WANDERER

I'm going to boil this fawn's bone.

It's going to shine again like light through a circle
of breath on a cold chapel window.

I might even take it back to the arroyo
for the New Year.
So it can wander back to the old cities
where it lived when the world was smaller,

when the longest grass blades tasted like milk.

Even then our human children grew like sweet red seeds
in the bitter corridors
of the pomegranate.

1.

They say William Bonnie hid
here behind the stones
of children lost to milk and lullabies.

He pressed his ear against their tiny
bones in yellow earth and sang,
anyway. If he killed men, he himself was not dead
to what stirred sparrows in night.

An oak branch promised him he would never hang,
so he crawled back to the old woman's house for supper.
She never called him Kid, or dirty
as a goat.

2.

Goatherd reported fifty Indians
hiding by the graveyard.
Women turned to coyotes,
dragged their pups into pianos,
cold ovens, root cellars.

Men turned to men with deer
rifles, shotguns, six-shooters,
cartridge belts and long bladed knives.

Walked towards the stone markers twinkling
in sun and shadow.
When they found the woods empty
there was a long silence, then
they all laughed at once,

like dead men surprised
at the sweetness of God.

They wanted to hang the goatherd.
Or at least make him suck the fallen tits
of a she-goat.

3.

Nowadays they say a crazy woman above the ghost
town planted these plastic chrysanthemums.

Hitchhiked to Silver City and mumbled
at that rancher the whole way. Prophesied

his cows would tell the old stories of greed and tired lust
because they were eating the grass
from shallow graves.
Maybe I'm that crazy woman, too.
One month after my wedding I tried out each
of the stones, their carved years,
their names.

Hung my circle wreath of baby's breath
on the fallen barbed wire fence
and laid down on the little beds

one by one, naked as grief,
that skinned coyote.

CHARLIE M^cCOMAS

1. *Red Beard*

They say he grew among them, into Red Beard.
He fought another for the sake of a woman
who stood slender as an oak
in hopeful light. When he lost, they buried
him where he fell. Beneath a slender oak,
without his grieving horse, or stones.

2. *Sierra Madre*

They say that May of 1938 an archeological expedition
into Mexico found a band of Apache
who'd escaped across the border half a century ago
when Geronimo surrendered at Skeleton Canyon. The newspaper reported
that Charlie was their red-haired leader,
his eyes like blue agates, old fire.

3. *Camp*

They say he did not live long,
though they gave him a mother and a name.
The U.S. army came to break the shelters
of ocotillo branches. They cut away

the shoulders of the mothers, like the wings
of dark swans, and pierced
the hearts of locust cradleboards to oaks.

A man who saw his mother fall
was cruel. Took a rock
and crushed the captive white boy's skull,

stepped out of Charlie's shadow like a ghost
who would not speak for one hundred and fourteen years:

Charlie, it is late, and I am sorry.

They say a fallen swan called out, *Son,*
and Charlie answered.

THE GREAT GREAT GRANDSONS

My wild son of fifteen Augusts
walked the San Francisco River.
Combing the grass
of the banks for return.
Scouting minnows.

Whistling for the ghosts of otter.

I was never afraid when he disappeared
among the cottonwoods.

Juniper smoke from the wood stove
and a bird mocking the shadow
of a mountain lion called him home.

Down river a man with a rifle in his hands
meets my long, brown son
at a fence that's strung across the river.

Best turn back, son.

I'm walking the river bottom.

Best turn back, son.

No one owns the river bottom.

Best turn back, son, because we do.

My slender son turned, swayed
by the waterweeds and the rifle
cutting a hole through the light.

Saw a female duck flounder to lure
chase, and wondered if this man
was just embarrassed. Lacked the animal grace
to kill a duck without a license.

But after that he walked up river,
towards the high-walled box where the water
runs too deep for wading.

Sometimes he went by flashlight
and pulled catfish so strong, even skinned
on the stringer, they plowed the water.

Brought them home to me.
And I was afraid,
of flashflood in the canyon,

of broken solitude,

of the holes in the light at the turn
of our century in this beloved country

where the great great grandsons of the trappers
can no longer walk the rivers,
those long and golden threads of cottonwoods.

Best turn back.

BILL EVANS LAKE, 1999

The last cold Sunday of the millenium
we fished among the waterweeds and the chamiso.

My son looked into the gold
jewel eye of the black duck
and the secret eye of the crane
and swore that he'd live, too.

I prayed every dark road in him
would lead to a place like this:

where he must have been before.

Not the two empty beers in an old fire.
Or the shirt sleeve the other boy cut away with a knife

so he could take a pure animal shit
behind the junipers.

Or maybe those, too.

I'm talking about deep water
ringed by mountains, and delighted
creatures staring back and willing to live

under the same sun, the same shadows.

4

SHADOW

Two thousand years since Christ was born
and the hawk still flies over the mountain.
I have seen him at dusk flying close to the ground
and I have loved him, even piercing
the shadow of the dove.

In the dove's shadow there's a garden.
In that garden there's a prayer, and
we live in that prayer
that begins and ends in blood.

TRADE

I traded my two diamond doves
for the interest on an old car
Irene at the landfill
sold for five-hundred dollars.

I didn't know Irene hated bird shit
and was sending my diamonds up the valley
to a blue-haired woman who didn't.

More than anything I've lost,
in this fourth decade of my life, I want,
I want my doves.

They were two night skies I felt
under my ribs.
Crowded with constellations.
And when they turned, they turned
and called together.

I turn towards my shadow
and a hawk flies out.

BURNING CAR

On 180 North out of Silver City,
that old car caught fire.

Before we saw smoke the dog leapt
from the open window at sixty miles an hour,
and waited for us in the brown
grasses beside the road.

We saw him in the rearview mirror
where the wooden cross he'd licked was hanging,
and got off that road, too.

My son and I stood watching as it blazed,

our feet surprised as wings.

Those caged birds who'd died, delicate
claws up in the charred backseat,

began singing again in the sweet air
off the highway,

among the goatshead
and the dried coyote gourd.

I come from people who would not forgive.

They were Spanish Protestants who ran like hell from Cortrai
to Holland and New Amsterdam,
damning the Inquisition,

and they were the Inquisition.

They were Puritans who painted their kitchens in Connecticut
and Massachusetts
the bright blue of angels, and led frail old women
to the gallows if their bones creaked against any trespass,

and they were also those cursing old women.

They were Scots and Welsh who dreamed their iron and arrows
like a thousand deaths of San Sebastian into the English army,

and they were the English army.

They were Indians, Potawatomi and Apache who nearly laughed
themselves to death
when they were taught to love their enemies,

and their enemies were also my people.

I too would rather laugh myself to death than die
at the hands of an enemy, even if he is my relative.

Or forgive anyone who's truly wronged me
or maybe only just slighted me
or anyone else in my family, or even a friend,

unless they're on their knees near my front porch
for at least one whole winter,
and even then, covered with sparrows.

And I am also those sparrows
and in this year of Nineteen Hundred and Ninety-nine,
I beg the Spirit of forgiveness to forgive me.

GIFT

In the dark rains last August they called Phillip to track
the bodies of two boys who were
horsing around in the Mimbres river.

Their mother looked down at a rainbow in her lamp,
and when she looked again, her boys were gone.

Maybe she threw that lamp into the river.
Gave the flood her light. Her rainbow. Her wedding band.
Any gift she could find to bargain with.

Turns out they washed out on a far bank way down the other side,
too far for calling,
but more alive than you or I.

They remembered they were holding hands
when they born again, like twins.

They spent the night among kind strangers,
men or bears who built them a great fire,

who showed them how to raise their hands
to greet the humans they warned would cry
when they saw them waving there.

YEAR OF LOVE AND DEATH

It was a year of love and death.
Across the San Simon Valley, the bare
mesquites were wreathed in doves,

and in Oklahoma the blue-eyed murderer
my wild sister slept with was taken by the Duncan sheriff,
her gloating ex-father-in-law,

and here at the mouth of this canyon
when the silver badged-voiced neighbors called to ask
about a pair of mountain lions they were hunting,

we lied. Stood in the big tracks
and said we saw no sign.

They found the Pueblo boy
in the spring,
only one mile from the camp

where the others had teased
him too hard for pride
about his missing deer.

He wore hunger like a pair of antlers,
sat and starved himself to death.
Stripped his soul
from his beautiful brown body.

These arrogant men, these goddamned
Irish and Indians who strip away
their hides in January

have burdened the place
between my heart and throat

with a disease like tuberculosis, only worse.

Sleep until the sand-hill cranes return.

Come spring,
think again of the smallest sorrow
in the vein

of the green leaf,
the smallest joy.

My son Joseph used to dream a bear
trying to open his small north window.

He wouldn't let it in because he thought it meant
to kill us, just when we'd figured out
how to weed two acres
of brown horehound
and burn dry tumbleweed

by whistling different tunes.

Now I dream that bear at Christmas.
He's scratching light on the walls of the sky
with a stick.

There's that bear and an evergreen
and there I am in this old red flannel nightgown.

When I wake up I'm standing at the stove.
Raising the old songs of the birds from the flaming juniper.

5

I had oak singing in the fire and the sun rising
over the purple east mountain.

A dog leaping over the clothesline
or running from big tumbleweeds.

I had a river that called
with turkey and cottonwoods.

I had blue heron and deer and javelinas
like somebody opened a box and they were the necklace.

One morning I looked out and I had a neighbor's seven dancing horses
shining in my dust.

I had a son for a brown coyote who could trick
a hawk into going to school on mornings
so cold they smoked.

I had a son who could trick a sparkling trout from the river
into my cast iron pan.

Once I gave him a gift like a mirror.
A pure rectangle of ice I broke from the laundry tub.

Every Christmas that coyote smiles and licks it
and hangs it in the evergreen branches of his favorite juniper.

FOX

Where there was nothing, a field.
Where there was January, a fire.
And where my soul was,
my beloved fox running,
his body a flame
I saw singing in the stove.

.

ROSE

O, Rose of the December light,
Holy Mother like a fox
who hears beneath the snow.

You who saw I was a woman without hooves,
without antlers, that for breasts I wore the broken
cups of fallen acorns.

On the longest night of my soul, You
led me into a house
in the Santa Rita pines,
and married me to a man like a bear.

He pointed at a green stick
and it blazed. When we were warm
we slept, and the fire shattered into the ochre

I dreamed that he painted on my bones.

1.

Wife with a violent man.
Took her to the barn to beat her
so the swallows could watch
from the rafters.

One day she got lucky as a red thread,
as a bottle of volcanic lineament oil,
and he was dead.

At the funeral, a black dog
like a man in a black cape came for the soul
in the pine box. A crowd shuddered,
and saw this.

2.

Woman with no horses. No house,
no acre of corn, no mother. No older
sister straight as a yucca against injustice.

Woman with a mirror. A water pitcher and basin.

And an uncle who says you will marry this man
I have chosen for you among the seeds
in steer dung of the best bulls.

Woman looks into the mirror and screams
until she breaks into so many brides,
the wedding is called off.

Maybe she lifted her veils and smiled
when they raised her into the horse cart
of the insane.

3.

Two springs ago, Father Kao shouting
the sons and daughters of Adam and Eve living
together as husband and wife, and not married
by the Church,
even if they have eight children,
are at the gates of hell.

I know something about raising babies, and if
they have eight children, they've passed through
that flaming door. From the back pew
my laughter crashes against the stained-glass windows
of the Church of San Lorenzo.

The old, the broken, the faithful, the afraid
are charred in that holy oven,
but my laughter escapes like a deer, carries me back
to the cool river.

In the churchyard I tell my red-faced husband,
that priest is evil.
I know Christ and he would break
Father Kao's flat nose.

DESIRE

Near the tin house
under the flap of the mountain's
long breast,

I screamed again for my husband,
then laid down between the rabbit brush
and the dry river stones
and saw winter clear to March.

I got so thin my sister swore
she saw me glittering
all the way to Oklahoma.

An old mountain lion was scavenging
her boiled chicken bones.
She called to say
it was screaming a sound like love
if that meant dying
to all but hunger.

The holy books I'm hiding from
tell about a hunger so pure
it can lift you straight to heaven.

Those books are liars.
That mountain lion never entered
the gates of heaven.

He went over a fence and was shot by a deaf neighbor,
who hid his silver bones in the red earth.

Of passionflower tea falls over my heart.

In the wet leaves at the bottom, there's a woman
leading a horse
through a marsh.

I see cattails like the ghosts of otter.

Sister, let's throw away our old clothes,
the dried hollyhocks,
these dry winds that call themselves
our husbands.

There's a wind that always guesses
where I'm sleeping in my truck on the road
to Oklahoma,

when I can't look at the Santa Rita mine
from our front porch anymore.

That wind must be my favorite husband
because he's always a red-tailed hawk

who circles three times
and turns me back South.

DEAD HORSE

I saw the dead horse in the canyon.
They said it was a torn paper bag the wind caught
on old bones.

They were liars who didn't want me
to raise seven dead horses.
To make them walk and rear up and run.

Tonight I am killing the horses again
in the thunder and the flood.
I'm killing them again with the thimble of pollen.

Once my dress was like a butterfly
around my hips. Raised for my birthright,
Love. Now I know that to be

a beautiful woman, and to live, to truly live,
means to become hammered gold.

Even when you lie down,
your husbands mistake you for the morning sun.
They spit on their hammers and call you very bad
luck, very bad luck.

NEST

The ghost of a nest of a cactus wren

cupped by six yellow fruits
of the cholla.

The oldest angels have manners,
they're not like the youngest birds.

I'm hollow-boned and wet-feathered.
I'm big-eyed and ugly.

One of the unlucky ones who live
the dead weight

of their ignorance

and depend on the same God
who can kill a deer with lightning.

I pray for the grace
of brown cactus wrens

who are not here.

To keep my appointment
with the sky. Never to break

my mother's delicate back.

III

MIRACLES OF SAINTED EARTH

I

FIRST HORSES, 1519

We were thrown into the sea
at the Horse Latitudes.

Our manes spit foam at the moon, our hooves
plowed salt from our lungs

until we heard the last syllable
of the grieving Arab's lullaby.

Then we rolled like opened wooden chests over
the black floor of the Atlantic,

we were death looking for a white sail.

Those of us who lived
went through the green door of a New World

where we were slaves.
Gentled men and women who'd forgotten
their own secrets.

We kept what we forgot
locked in our eyes and we rode into cornfields,

into war, under the heavy thighs
of men we wore like silver idols.

Among the first laws of New Spain, it was ordained
no Indian could ride us.

We heard them tell the Indians we were immortal.

That we were the lower part of a riding God,

and they must build corrals to hold us back

from devouring their human flesh.

The Indians watched our captors ride us with saddles
inlaid with silver and gold,

watched as our captors slept with us like silken women,
ran their tongues over the lashes of our velvet eyes,
made us beds next to their own.

The Indians went to war with us.

They burned us alive, or filled
us with arrows and ate the flesh from our necks
and left us among the gramma grasses.

When the first Apache chose one of our fastest
and rode away into thorns and pink hills,

the enemies of our enemies became our friends.

We loved those men who spoke into our manes
with sounds that had no word for king

and many for wind.

They sweated on us and rubbed our sweat
onto their bodies
until we were one.

They raced us and cast cords around our necks.

When winter weakened us they trapped us
in canyons or against bluffs

where our eyes rolled with the memory of salt waves.

They breathed into our nostrils until our spirits mingled,
and we gave them our speed and flesh
in exchange for their language
of wind.

Later, the horse-whisperers stepped forward, they were men
who were horses, too, of all colors. We chose them

for our healers, we
made them forget they were men
whose descendants would be born
inside fences, hospitals.

They almost made us forget the lightless bottom of the sea,
where our deaths are still calling like white sails.

CIBOLA

I was gold and I was not there.
I was burning under pale Spanish skin,

I was a hope for noble husbands for seven
starched crows, pious daughters in Mexico City.

I made men who penned stylish Castilian ballads
eat lizards and pick the seeds out of coyote dung.

I shed their skins like the ghosts of snakes
under the sun of New Spain

and still I was loved like an afterworld,

more than grass or rain,
or a naked woman in beds of myrrh.
The Franciscan friar Marcos de Niza desired

me in the shape of a true cross, a northern river valley
to lay at the feet of the Bishop of Mexico. He desired me

for five golden corks to stop the flowing blood from the wounds
of Jesus Christ Our Savior.

On his journey north he saw me in the distance
after I threw down the ceremonial gourd
of copper bells and killed

the Moor slave Estevanico
and his Indian friends. The friar in his brown robe
saw me in the smallest of seven cities

and named it the new kingdom of St. Francis.
He piled twenty dusty stones around a juniper
cross, and claimed it in the name of an Emperor

who had a passion for the lives of broken
clocks, mice, doves.

But I was not there. I was choking with laughter,
like a horse gasping for breath,

in my underground chairs in far off hills,
and in those quiet shipwrecked rooms

under the wide skirts of my true love, the blue sea.

THE BLUE LADY, 1635

I, Sister Maria de Jesus de Agreda
made five hundred blessed journeys to New Spain

to bring the word of Christ
to people brown as Our Lord's sparrows.

On my flights I took them rosaries, gathered splinters
in my palms when I planted His crosses

near that river that echoed the glory
of Our Savior's body.

They called me the Blue Lady because I wore
the sackcloth of our Order

like a patch of sky that flowed
among yellow cottonwoods.

The Lord sent me without a horse,
without the swords of Toledo.

It often happened at this very table. I lifted the bread
to my mouth and saw angels. I was standing in that other

country speaking in tongues I cannot speak
here at the border of Castile and Aragon.

I saw my duty sweet as the fold of a dove's wing.
I was martyred many times, my wounds

blessed by my angels. I saw you, Fray Alonso,
baptize the pueblos of Piro.

I saw a bead of sweat
sting your eye and join the holy water.

I saw Fray Juan de Salas and Fray Diego Lopez
and the poor Indians I sent to them from Isleta,
the painting in the refectory
of our Mother Luisa de Carrión.

I turned the Indians towards you desert fathers.
Once at the door of the church I administered

a gentle shove to a crowd that caused much laughter.
They are a joyous people, even stumbling.

They weave bright necklaces of winter jasmine
for the True Cross that lights the mourning

veils of Spain. I have prayed for harmony between
the governors and you friars. I have prayed for

swords and arrows to return to water.
I will say nothing of my three-hundred-year-old

body that refuses to corrupt in this glass coffin. Hear that Spanish
and Indian must be one prayer, the two wings

of the same Inca dove.

CORNFIELDS

We lived along these rivers
they later named for their saint who preached

to trout and crows, and for all their Holy Saints,

and in the canyon they named for their holy woman
who tore out her own eyes.

San Francisco, Todos Santos, Santa Lucia.

Father Bartholome saw us with his band
of three hundred in 1756.

We were the true gold of these gentle hills.

Foxes lived among us and caught our playing mice
in their sharp mouths. We asked only to let live.
To wave under the wind near the laughter
of children who might be carried away in the basket
of a coyote the color of ashes.

We are a sign against war.
A sign against fear.

We disappeared when those who raised
us ran away into the mountains.
We never asked for blood.

We asked for butterflies,
those women who could run with fleetness.

Strong mothers who could gather
the first light's pollen.

WHIPPOORWILL

It was the whippoorwill, the night bird
our People called Ja-jo, bathing in the dust of the road.

I listened to him even though it was told
I would fall into a fire or a river, or a bad thing

would happen to someone I loved. I wanted
to spy on God, not mind my elders. So the evil whippoorwill
raised me to the horse of a Spanish soldier, sold me south
to Mexico City to people who barked when they talked.

On the long walk of my dream I saw
my mother burn her grief away from her forehead

with a hot knife, tell my father she would go
without Christ forever.

Less than a year, the dog strangers caught
the tiny boy who fell from between my thighs.

I was twelve springs old. I don't know if I loved him.
I called him Ja-jo. I bathed him in dust and I laughed
when he sang his evening song.

My song will kill those Mexican guards.

I'm on my hands and knees in a dark hole.
Hammering the stone breasts of our Holy Mother Earth
to shining bits I pour in rawhide.

I kill Don Elegea and his grant from the Spanish crown
with a high note. I shatter his thick mud walls.

I lay our broken Mother across my back and climb out on the pole
notched for a chicken's feet.

In the light I see the free ones watching from those hills.

Don Elegea, my low note: in one year your wife will be a widow
who will ride her own sons
like black horses in your bed.

The free ones watch from the eyes of their stolen horses
and turn softly away.

To the east I have seen lightning in a tree signal them
to trample my chest and the long testicles of these Mexicans.

But out of sight the free ones run
from this red dust that is a death song on my face
and on my fingernails.

Don Elegea, I feel a sharp pain in your left side.

I am the skeleton you will find in one hundred years
when the glory hole swallows the three towers
of the old fort prison.

I died when our Mother threw her old body
over me. This was a miracle of sainted earth.
I didn't call out once. I opened my eyes
and smiled in my live burial.

Once we were saints, not ghosts, on this river.
We leapt one thousand times over the yelping coyote's back
until he ran for cover.

We were tender with our own. Tucking them like brown nests
among the cattails
and reading the tracks of wolves and lions in the wind
through old cottonwoods.

We lived through centuries, more joy than the sun's tassels
in rusted traps sprung on the heaviness
of rotten leaves.

The rivers flowed with fish whose bodies held the mysteries
of God's blindness. We ate those fish and would not see
the time of gentleness was over.

We await our resurrection in the wild
eyes of the Holy One.

SANTA RITA MASSACRE, 1837

They said it would be a feast,
they said it would be a massacre.

They said it would be friendship,
they said it would be a famous lie fit for a play
to be performed for the President.

They said it would be whisky, sugar, flour and ground corn,
they said it would be cannon, nails, metal, muskets, knives.

They said the women would stand strong and virtuous
in their bean and seed necklaces,
they said the fallen cradle boards would run
with the blood of Missouri rifles.

They said James Johnson of Kentucky
was a friend of old Juan José.
They said Johnson hunted scalps for the gold of Chihuahua.
That he would hack that happy drunk
Indian to death with two knives.
They say twenty fell,
they say it was four hundred.

That Mangas Coloradas leapt the wall of the presidio
with a baby in his arms.
That those who ran away were deer or antelope.
I was a fallen seed in a hoof print
among the shattered bowls of cornmeal,

and I never saw their brown legs
touch the ground.

NO DEVIL IN A BLACK CAPE, 1842

Our father sat under his grandfather's olive tree
near the garden wall on Sundays.
There he almost remembered Spain.

Our mother kept the Holy Faith of New Mexico
like silver needles in a rosewood box.
She taught my sisters and I to embroider with the black
silk strands of our hair on handkerchiefs.

Why I turned towards the river or did not care to be pure I do not know.
There was a scent of deer from the broken cottonwoods.
There was my own shadow like red wine falling among the white goats.

My brothers wanted permission to take their knives to kill the Texans
who were trying to spread their lawless country up our valley.

Through the time of apple blossoms, Father only opened
his mouth to eat. Then one morning he carried an axe to his beloved olive.

When it fell, Mother was on her knees. My two brothers took one horse,
led it through our wooden gate. Waved from the South.

Six years later their horse returned, mounted by a gentle golden-haired
man who stopped to ask for water. I spit in it. Father died that night
while the priest was north, in San Miguel.

Even after I married I never wanted my husband
as much as I wanted my secret on the stubble of the river.

I built a grotto there. Luis would not forgive.
My children buried me here in the churchyard.

They made me beautiful in my wedding dress and garlands of wild flowers.
I was forgotten by the devil who never appeared in his black cape.

FORT BAYARD

They raised the dust and hid themselves and seven hundred horses.
I never wanted glory after I saw that sweet Irish wash girl
fighting my shirt into a horsetrough.

I chased Indians some told were only men towards Old Mexico.
Valleys too lonely for a hawk's shadow.

There I looked at jackrabbits and smelled towns
going up straight along creeks. Pine board houses
of God where a man could rest clean in this wilderness.

I didn't believe too much in gold.
I believed and fought for the Union.

When I had to kill I killed quickly. I'd never killed in County Cork.
I believed in work, and most of all, in water.
I wanted to marry that Cavan girl and her bathing our children
in stories by firelight. I wanted to send a letter across the sea
Father Danaugh in Ireland could read
to my father, and fifty dollars for him.

I never wanted this silence. Here under the poison roots
of this spreading yellow-flowered whore. Creosote who reaches for me
under my forgotten pile of stones.

DUST STORM

I was raised with the help of a Spirit who loves them.
I hide one thousand Apaches in the year 1873.
They speak through me.

We have never been commanded to love our enemies.
We have chosen to take heart for heart
because we have been murdered on quiet mornings
when we were innocent with the hope of green hummingbirds
in tall agaves.

We have never seen Christ or the Blue Lady.

Those Mexicans were made to be stolen from
since the time their grandfathers raised their bloody pyramids
and took us to Azatlan in cages.

Seven years ago Americans cut off the head of Mangas
who offered to lead them to gold.
They boiled the head and sent it to Washington.

We don't want to hear about those schools too far
East where our children will learn
to read tuberculosis.
One in ten of us lives. We are all in mourning

and we will fight until the last of their wagons
disappears into the blood
of the rising sun.

BLUE WILLOW, 1870

When I left Missouri Mother tucked her grandmother's Blue Willow
plate into the wedding ring quilt.

Eighteen years I never saw her cry, but that morning she shook
like snow from a small pine
two ravens fly away from.

This cabin's cold, she said, but we have to be careful with our wood, and
turned away
to look at my four little sisters sleeping on their feather tick.

I grabbed her elbow and began to cry. She held me against her neck.
It smelled like mint and had a feel I promised the small sun
on my back I would never forget.
When I climbed into the wagon beside my husband,
she handed me her plate in this quilt.

Once she said my eyes are our plate's color. My grandmother and my
mother and my sisters we were all born with dark blue eyes
with patterns like this.

We've got whole stories in them with only men to talk to, or the pines
when the men are off chasing turkeys or deer.

We talk to ourselves and don't mind. It's like a prayer we don't stop.

I heard about a blacksmith over in Texas who fell to his knees
and died talking for four days about that war with Mexico.

We women aren't built that way.
We hold things more softly, so we can hold them longer.

Like this china going over the prairies and the rocks of shallow streams.
I won't let it break because it was my mother's and it's been in England
and in Pike County, Pennsylvania and Missouri.

In the plate there's a castle like a cabin in the forest next to a blue willow
that rises over a river. That's where we're going.

Maybe we'll cross the same bridge as Hong Shee and Chang
in the Blue Willow plate's old story.
She found a letter in a paper boat he sailed asking her to run away.
He was her father's secretary, smart as horses. They escaped, but a storm
turned over their boat and God helped them become two birds.

We go through a valley.
Women don't break. They turn to doves.
They turn their men to doves and the two go free
above these yellow grasses.

BROTHEL

I was a whore. Men came to me like going
to church. They called on God between my legs and got
a good night's sleep.

They say whores don't like the act, but when they came
to it young and clean, they found me
smiling. I got their money. Sometimes they left
their guns instead. Or a gold necklace. Or a deed

to one hundred wild acres they won in a card game
and didn't want to ranch.

Mostly, they had honor. After an hour of talk they wanted
to get married. Or their wives to come from back East.

Or just unlock the bedroom door those poor women
in Silver City closed against the grief of babies
in the cemetery.

Sometimes they slept and had very good or very bad
dreams. One was hanged. Another made a fortune
in Georgetown and got back to his West Virginia County.

Nights I got to be alone, all I wanted was the smell
of streams.

Then I counted my money.
The bed sweated of tired horses no matter how
often I sent the sheets to Hong Lee.
I hated sidewalks.
I hated being invisible to decent families.

I hated whisky in the mornings before I opened my eyes
to the painted tin ceiling.
I hated Millie, that golden bitch with the soul of a crowded city.
She'd sell her own
twelve year-old sister to a federal judge
because she hated anything that was just
itself, untouched.

That's why I've been living in this valley.
Why I was a woman out here ranching. I always paid
the men who built my fences, ran my herds to town.
Paid them well. They tried, but I never married.

I took a daughter whose family fell to influenza.
I sent her East to school, with a trunk of books and white dresses.

Since I died, no one has visited except the wind
at this ivory stone that no longer bears my name.
This is the good clear solitude I wanted.

Dear God, I hear they are calling
me Tan Wolf, and I am glad because I am tired of being
General George Crook.
Chasing the wind on my mule, Apache.

My own complain I am melancholy, that I never wear
my uniform, but I have been your faithful servant.

I looked for your boy Custer in the Montana wilderness.

If I ever forgot my duty, it was only because I landed
seventy trout from Goose Creek that evening.

Or I got sidetracked by the glorious birds' eggs in nests
you planted to lure us west of the Mississippi.

A soldier can fight
but never hate men who are not cowards.
Lord, I am only logic. Your blue machine
against the Apache.
This Pit River arrowhead has lived in my right
hip for twenty years. It's good
company, and smarter than my officers.
But not as smart as my wife, that woman you gave the secrets
of milk and fire.

This morning I want to hunt the brightness of one more wild
turkey while these prissy officers curse me
in their diaries.

Then I'll pray once again to be the irony
on the smiles of my adversaries.

3

DRAGOONS, 1874

I am the silence of a horse next to the body of Cochise.
Dead, he sat astride me with another riding warrior.

At the jagged crevice, they raised a gun to my head
and I fell into burial.
I welcomed his rifle-shotgun inlaid with silver and gold, his dog.

When he reached me through the spider threads of lowered ropes
I did not grieve. Four days we heard the lamentations,
the howl of our one thousand in the camp
of their great heart deepening the ravines.

Then we were born together.
We rose on the ochre-painted bones
of this wind that has no name.

Those do-goods smiled me into this horse cart
of crazies bound for California.

I thanked them for it
and turned away. Good manners only get a man
so far. First chance I get, Tucson, I'm jumping off.

I've got names, addresses.

After I told it fifty times
I told it fifty more. I was only afoot after a desert fox,

she was the first to find that mail driver killed.

As many arrows as a saguaro but he just sat there looking
like the sky had shown us both a mirror.
Looked like they took the horses, threw down the boxes, opened
them and rifled for anything they wanted.

Saw no use for letters so the wind had second shot.
Letters filled the road like little paper birds.
Most clawed stones and flocked around junipers.
Some were making it over the grasses
towards a bluff.

Those humble birds were a sign from God.
I made our good Lord the promise I'd read and remember
every one, in case I met the person it was
addressed to.

I set up camp. Took me two months to learn the five hundred
stories I gathered. None went
over the bluff.

I got the names straight so I could rattle
them off quickly.

I don't know and I don't care about any laws.

That mail driver was good company.
But now he's dead, and I won't stop looking
for the rightful owners of the white birds I carry
in my head.

THIS SKY

That first year I stared into those brown foothills.
An owl that flew in daylight tore out my heart
with sharp claws.
Carried it that way, dropped it.
I made it back to this cabin, fast
as a wild rabbit.

Sometimes I panted so hard it began to rain.
The arroyos ran gray and free like coyotes.
Turkeys stared into the river in the sky.

I'd never seen lightning look so much like war.
I made up prayers that felt like the empty nests
of cactus wrens.

I wasn't the only scared woman in this valley,
but I cried because being a newcomer here
felt like dying.
I was being washed clean.
The old folks told me I'd be born again in the pale trumpets
of the desert willow in May.

But when the mists of November came I fell to my knees.
I believed in all I saw and in all I could not see.

There was no more hiding.
I saw I'd never go back East, even for a funeral, an inheritance.

I wrote them a letter asking for the moist roots
of the hardiest roses. Slender branches
of apples, pears, almonds.

They're Episcopalian, but I told them I'd seen this great world
was just a church when the sky takes away
the doors, the walls.

They answered twenty years later. The neighbors
brought their letter here to my place under the willow
and read it aloud.

I was dead of cholera but I heard the blood voices
of anger and grief still blaming me for all
I had not loved.
I turned away and made no answer.
I damned them with this sky that is forever.

LOZEN

My gift came from God for the good
of my people. I lifted my hands to the sky.
I looked up and prayed, searching for our enemies.
I saw as one sees from a height, in every direction.

I turned in a circle until a humming like bees
stung my palms.

If they turned purple, the Mexicans,
the white men, the black men who wanted to kill us were near.
I calculated their distance. We acted accordingly.

I led men across flooded rivers.
James Kaywaykla remembers how I struck the shoulder of my horse
with a foot like lightning and men followed.

Even now I want to hide when a wind shouts my name,
but this is how we lived.
I went with the warriors as their sister.

Our clothes turned to rags.
All that we had was left behind.

I never married.
If I loved that Gray Ghost.
If I loved that chief of the Seneca who wandered,
looking for a land for his people,
that was only a door into this mountain.

It was not this mountain. Once inside, I thought
of that gray wolf only in that hour when the light was brown
as those lilies hidden in his face.

WALK HOME FROM MEXICO CITY, 1880

We five women disappeared at Tres Castillos
in the blazing desert crowned with rattlesnakes
among one-hundred and forty-six
of our dead and captured.

It was not those Mexicans who killed Victorio.
Even if they paid their Tarahumara scout
two thousand pesos and a nickel-plated rifle.

We saw that Victorio fought
until his cartridges were gone,
then turned his knife towards himself.

When the battle was over we were
slaves. Carried far past
the Blue Mountains. When the prickly pear
bore fruit, we crept away from the hacienda.

We five women shared one blanket
and one knife. We walked north, giving
thanks for every thorned sweetness
until we saw the mountains of Chihuahua.

We came into a town on the Cañada Alamosa
and American soldiers there took us in a wagon
to our people at Turkey Creek.

They will say the journey was a thousand miles
as the crow flies. As we traveled, many more.
They will say that after the journey
we were more than women.

They'll say we were the raging torrents
of rain through desert canyons.
That lightning put on her shoes and walked
north, then east, making holy ground.

SMALL MOCCASINS

Because I was a Christian
I sank the cradleboard with a stone in the river
and made my way back to the house
in the shade of the baby's black eyes.

She watched me like a naked owl
from her nest in the corner as I hid
her tiny moccasins away in the chest my grandmother's
grandmother brought from Spain. Remember, I said
to her, and then forget.
In twenty years your own daughter will be born.
Your man will be gentle, like mine.
Proud to walk harnessed to a plow,
just one step behind the sun.

I'll be a grandmother then, and I'll just pretend
I found these small moccasins.
We'll fish your daughter from her cradle
and put them on.
I'll say they were a gift
from a courageous woman I knew long before
my hair turned silver as a knife.

That woman must have been
my friend, because she burned her heart out like
an oak stump, and hid her child
inside the lightning of this history.

RAIN

I'll fall where I damn well please.

And I please over the wild grasses and their doves.
Over cornfields, and horses that are padlocked,
and horses carrying away their own thieves.

Over mesquite, orchards.
Jails, cemeteries, banks, sidewalks, gallows.
Valleys wide as summer.

Over the candlelit dinners of the governors
and the dark camps of fugitives. Over murder, and birth.

Over the tall straight lines of clapboard houses.
Like whiskey on the faces of good women.

Because I'm against chastity. Against holding out, playing
favorites. I'm for the desert crocus that opens to any
hummingbird's clear passion.

4

I had no mother.
I was born to a hollow stump.
She couldn't hold rainwater.
As far as she saw it, the female duty was to avoid
loving anything too much.

Never open the waterfall inside your chest, even when it crashed
like God's own music
under the starched fabric of your high-necked dress.

Mother fought to keep my hands off the piano keys
and in the bread dough or the sewing basket.

Nights I pressed against the hell of my black angel.
We filled the house with thunder, lightning.
We were my mother's nightmare.
She turned away the scholarship they offered from the conservatory.

Announced my engagement to a boy who'd grimaced at me
over tea and cookies.
Told me I'd never be a beautiful lady or an exceptional wife,
but if I tried hard I could please this clerk.
That I could give birth to angels if I could do it without screaming.

Night in the parlor I stared into the oval glass portrait of my mother,
her thick hair piled away from her angelical face.
Her blue eyes and mouth gentle with suffering.
Her waist cinched too tight for running if our house caught fire,
and saw myself.

I saw how cruel it was to volunteer for sainthood.

I wanted to tear the flesh from saints' bones.
Strip away my dress.
Let my hair tangle down my back in the frizz I'd always flattened
on the ironing board.
I wanted to be a running, sweating mare.

In the dark I heard my piano breathe and stamp
and I saw it wasn't an angel but a black horse.
All that I had left of my father besides a funeral card embossed
with an ivory column.
One week later I'd freed my stallion,
had it shipped by train to Santa Fe.
We made the journey south to this little mining town.
They wanted it in the saloon, they let me play anything
I wanted as long as it was wild.

The owner explained the music had to make customers feel
like they were being chased through dust and winning.
We understood each other.
Now they've made a law to keep women out of the saloons.
I don't blame them. Prostitution's bad as marriage.
I've only seen unhappiness. Women whose faces look like racetracks
for someone else's horses.

So George cut a hole in the wall and turned the piano
so I could sit outside. Play it into the saloon. I'm just as happy.
He's not breaking the law and I'm still riding the keys.

With the sun and the wind and the dark and one million
stars winning their race over me.

I gave mine to that woman and her boy
because God doesn't give that saint the dove anything more
than a nest on the ground.

I haven't lost my faith in Him completely.
I've looked for Jesus and I've seen striped fawns
torn exactly in four by a mountain lion.

Bones in every direction except the one my heart took over that trail
the cat licked clean.
Sometimes I've put bones back together, nestled a clump
of purple verbena against them.

Fifty years old and I've never married.
But I've never abandoned a woman.
I've spent my life away from towns, half of it looking for gold.

I've never killed a man. Those two times we took our sticks
of dynamite and jerky and went our separate ways
in the hills.

There's something about a woman alone with a child
that's like a deer and her fawn.
Maybe it's the cautious eyes. Or maybe it's the long rosemilk
you know their breasts are even when they're sweeping
rattlesnakes out of the kitchen.
Or picking up a dead husband's rifle to greet a hungry stranger.

I've seen women spread dishes on tablecloths draped
over oak stumps.
Make wise-ass boys pray, work and read in mining camps
men tripped and went straight to hell in.
I've seen women steady as oil lamps on nights
that resurrected bears.
Seen them lay the dead down and raise those who had
only one foot out of the coffin.

All for nothing except something God put inside
them like a meadow of coneflowers.

It was the smile in her eyes like water from a well
when she handed me that hot cup of coffee.
Her shy boy spying from behind the small woodpile.

I left my gold at that well. Not so that I could go back
for a drink. But half so I could have the memory of astonished good
fortune on a humble woman's face.

Half because holding that gold meant the beginning
of the end.
It meant business partners, fine suits, noisy suppers
under chandeliers.

It meant hundreds of strangers with their laughters and greeds
and pretendings,
each one more like the last.

When I looked again into these hills I saw the true gold,
the wandering without end.

That night I dreamed my mother knelt over me, dabbing starlight
with a rag on a wound in my chest.
She died as I was born. But not before she spent that winter taming
a pregnant doe with corn.
She was half-Chippewa and saw her death coming
over the lake in Canada.
My twelve year old sister raised me on that doe's milk.

Morning light showed deer prints in my camp.
None leading away.

BUFFALO SOLDIER

We were ten years old the day my father told my twin
brother and me we were no longer slaves, but free.

That night in our cabin over a bright candle flame we saw
our parents read the stories of Paradise in each other's eyes.

We spied. Heard our mother pronounce the words
"I want" aloud for the first time.

Saw our father deepen with pride. Grow like a South Carolina
night where we were all safe, asleep.

White neighbors hid their faces and they hung him
anyway, because he bought forty good acres on the river.

Mother cut the rope but it was too late.
Sat in a chair and rocked him all night. Buried him in a length
of red silk a pretty sister turned prostitute gave her.

Our crop died tall in the field.
Nights my twin Joseph and I stole chickens, anything
that would go into a cookpot. Sixteen, we lit out to Oklahoma.

Tried our hands at cowboy. Decided to soldier
instead since we wanted the glory.

Yesterday a whiskied son of an Irishman here at Fort Bayard
drew his pistol and killed my brother
because he couldn't bear the sight of a black
man in a fine uniform.
I rode away when that soldier went unpunished.

I laid in wait. Like a rattlesnake. Like the hiss of God
under a rock. I got justice, and slid away. Made it look like Indians.

I went home. Passed for a Christian, and maybe I was.
I pretended I was my dead brother.

Mother told us apart by a rabbit's foot on a silver chain
she gave Joseph because he smiled more than I did.
He was her favorite.

I smiled, and wore that chain until they laid me in the earth,
thirty years later, under a cross they painted
with my murdered brother's name.

I was a black woman named Annie.
They hung my husband in Fort Worth because he stood straight,
looked those Texans in the eye
and asked for his money when they owed him for work.

He was born to a fieldworker on a plantation
and no man ever treated me better.
I dug up the rosebush Lucas planted for me,
gathered our four children, took them West

to New Mexico Territory.

We kept the roots of the rosebush moist, over the grasses,
the desert. We watered it with our tears, good as a river.

My children are Lucas' and my wedding day,
just multiplied by four.
We lived in a tent while I did chores in the mining camp in Kingston.
I scrubbed and baked, killed chickens, helped women
have their babies. Saved every dollar

I earned in a biscuit tin I hid
in a hollow juniper because they're never struck by lightning.
I fed our children on stringy rabbits I baked tender
with vegetables from our garden. I made them pies
from the red thorned fruit of the prickly pear.

I doctored them with medicines I found growing in the canyons,
tall purple coneflowers and mint like heaven Lucas came back
to help me gather.
Sometimes we held hands and once he tried to love me
in the old way, and couldn't, because he was an angel now.

He sat crying in the shade of a granny sycamore until she covered
him with a quilt of falling yellow stars.

He got a good sleep and when I returned
his face had lost its blue and the red mark had disappeared

from his fine neck. He shook off the leaves like a wind,
like a shining black wolf. I promised him that a woman
as busy as I was didn't have time to think about wrapping her legs
around a man's hips, anyway.

My bank in the juniper earned me a house
made of pine boards down the gulch from Kingston.
I set the rosebush in the ground, and there I raised
our children, but I never stopped meeting my husband

in the canyon. It was like a black wolf with sweet breath.
It was like holding hands with purple dawns, sunsets.
Never cold. Sometimes he even sweated and I could smell
his salt in the wind.

When those Texas rawhiders came to Kingston, he told me,
They're going to try to kill you.
He gave his life once and he wanted to give it again.
I stalked off that day, angry as hell about men being noble.

That night there was the knock on the door
and our four children started blowing snot and tears
through their noses.
I told them to steady their chins, Lucas.
That God is good even when his creatures aren't.

I told the knock I'd light a lamp, put on a dress.

There were fifty of them in a circle about the house, mostly
rawhiders. I talked to the mine superintendent, Mr. Hadley,
and Mr. Jimmie McKenna. I invited them in
and told the forty-eight no-account Texans hiding their rope

they could stay outside.

The two men were looking for little Mandy Lou,
who our young ones had seen pulling a burro's tail
in front of her Mama Annabelle's restaurant that afternoon.
I wasn't hiding her bones in my laundry basket.

I didn't want the spilled blood of a child the color of roses and sour milk.

They left, posted two miners with rifles to guard us against
the Texans until morning.

Sunrise, Mrs. Annabelle cantered back on a borrowed horse,
Mandy Lou smiling in her arms. All night the burros had circled
the girl, biting, kicking hard to defend her, kept her walking
a nightmare in the frost.

Because of wolves.
The tracks told everything.

If not for wolves, Lucas, that innocent would have died
of exposure. Husband, you had a long night.
The Texans trapped the others, twenty dollars a pelt,
but they won't take you again. Take my hand. It's so pretty
in this canyon where the best medicines are.

BECAUSE THEY WERE HUNGRY

My mother never had a biscuit for any man
on a warpath. She loaded a rifle, made me
hide in a cold oven.
But when they came in peace,
she fed the Apache.
Because they were hungry. Then, we're all alike,
she explained as she hung our calico dresses
like waving meadows of paintbrush on the clothesline.
Souls is what we are, and our bodies
are like these dresses that are filled
with the breath of the wind for a while.
Do good while you're here.
Before you're laid in that pine box.
Child, when you're at the door to Heaven
the question the tallest angel will ask you is:
did you ever let anyone go hungry?

If you did, your heart will weigh too much
for those brand new wings that are like a blue heron's.
From then on you'll have to be one of those lonely
catfish, big as a cabin, that lives
at the bottom of the lake
we left behind in Missouri.

CIGARETTE

A cigarette held three lives at Tres Castillos,
after the massacre by the Mexican soldiers.
An Indian mother and her small boy waited
for dark and crawled away.

They lay in a crevice shallow as their breath
while the stars shone like blades through
the dark roots of their hair.
Only a few feet from a Mexican soldier

rolling a cigarette.

They watched him smoke it. It made clouds
that covered his face so that the loving woman
beautiful as a brown wolf
almost leapt to make him a ghost

with her knife.

But I, that baby who became James Kaywaykla,
was in the way. The soldier crushed
the charred butt with the heel of his boot and strode away.
And my mother and I crept away from our Death, too.

We escaped it through a veil of thorns and night.

JUST MEXICANS

The earth swallowed my father
and my brothers. When they cried out to be
saved, only the ravens answered.
They met Christ like a swallow of stinking vinegar.
Word got to my mother, Amparo, and she borrowed
a horse and wagon.

The lines in her face deepened into roads
as we flew towards the mineshaft.

The white boss told our cousin who translated it
would have been useless digging men out
of good, deep graves.

Mother raked his face and the red earth
until her nails were broken claws and her Spanish failed.
They carried her away to San Lorenzo,
my grandparents' little house of adobe on the river.

Pure white chickens and appleblossoms met us
at the door with young souls.
It was Easter.

In the churchyard there was a boy
named Patrick O'Riley with eyes blue as the Virgin's mantle,
and he said we could play house, but never
be married. I was ten years old but I heard it
was because we were just Mexicans.

5

I was only sorry to leave that rosebush I planted
and named Alma,
just off my porch on Yankee Street.

Silver City was a town of strangers who lived in perpetual
night, even when the sun was shining.

Far as I saw, men didn't work. They plotted. How to win
a race, a fight, a card game, a cow. Even beans.

Or better, trick a brother or a longtime friend
into doing it for them.

If they were given one hundred good acres on the river,
they didn't raise anything but a bottle
to their unshaved chins.

Right there on the little path between the irises and hollyhocks
I saw hangings in those oaks.
Bets called on where the dead would go.

I called to children but they ran wild. Weren't taught
to obey, to work.
If a man could read he was reviled, worse if he was honest.

Women like me, raised to keep her female beauty to her husband,
had words thrown like gravel sting her face
on the sidewalk.

I was handsome but I didn't wear bright
red, or the thin veils of a temptress and my Cyrus was gone
unless the sun was high.

I had the thin comfort of the Scriptures at night.

I followed Cyrus to that godforgotten town
because we were just married. He promised we'd find gold
and send some back to my parents on their West Virginia farm.

It took me twenty years to get our first child.
I was forty when I placed my hand on my belly and felt the true gold
of these barren hills.

I pinned a rose from Alma to my travelling dress
and wept on her branches when I told her good-bye.

I took the stagecoach to Lordsburg.
The train back to my valley in the East. My valley of lonely violins,
humble laughter and whippoorwills.

Dear Father, I like this place.
Mrs. Pratt is writing you this letter.

When we first came they cut our hair. We cried all night
because we thought someone had died.

We have a farm. Our shoes hurt our feet.
We drink cold water. My sisters are trying to breathe
in their new dresses.

I am learning to build with wood and a hammer.
Everyone is good here. A Negro boy was killed on the railroad.
Please send my bow and arrows.

We go to church on Sundays and I wear a blue suit.
A Cheyenne boy shot himself.
Write to tell me if you have horses again, and how is

my sister White Sky who got married. And how are
my uncles and grandfather at Fort Sill.
Please send my bow and spiked arrows.

Here we have green grass where we kick a football. There is a cemetery.
We have good teachers.

We don't speak Apache because now we speak English.
We learned not to spit when it lightnings.
I want to see you again and be together. Geronimo talked

in the parade. The Lord made his heart good.
In two years Mr. Pratt says I can come home if I learn.
I have a bed to myself. Sometimes at night the stars I watch

look at me sleeping. I dreamed you sent my bow and arrows.

DEATH SONG, RODEO, 1905

It was time to die so I walked back to where I was born
seventy-five years ago,

to where my umbilical cord
was buried in the hoof print of an antelope.

My mother and my aunts were gathering acorns.

My father riding across the border into Mexico,
and just returned with horses, saddles and blankets
colored like rainbows.

I was playing lookout with my cousins and practicing war
on an innocent tarantula
who was our prisoner.

My sisters ran their races good as deer. When we hid until dark
Grandmother threatened us with the coyote and his basket
and the whippoorwill.

The cottonwoods turned gold.
When my father raided and found silver, he left it there,
on the ground.

It was time to die so I returned.
To the valley near the Canyon of the Skeletons where our warriors
agreed to stop fighting.

I saw the springs gone dry. The cottonwoods like broken necklaces.
The miles of gramma grasses I thought to hide in were gone.

Where they had been was a dried lake of mesquite and thorns,
and a town called Rodeo.

I kept my road, my eyes fixed ahead.
When they saw me, when they raised their rifles and whistled

death my way, I was singing. It was my own death. It was my own song,
and it was a good one.

THE RETURN, 1913

April, we Chiricahua were freed
from our twenty-seven years as prisoners.

We rode the train to Mescalero.
Beyond the screen of dust we felt the place
of black jagged rock we once crossed to the west.

When we got to the platform, our dogs we'd been forbidden
to take leapt from beneath our blankets and shirts
and barked all our happiness.

The Mescaleros greeted us in Tularosa.
They gave us food, and we tried not to laugh
at how they spoke Apache.

Then we traveled north for twenty miles in wagons.
We saw yucca, mesquite. We saw our warriors too,
and tried not to call back their ghosts
with our tears.

We settled at White Tail, the place our friends gave us.
It was high, an eight-mile valley crossed by streams.

There was a fire and our crop burned
in the field. My father hunted deer. My mother and I gathered
the seeds of grasses, wild onions and Indian spinach.

We waited four years for the houses
they promised us. Winter was too long in the barn
and my mother died of pneumonia.
Grandmother cut my hair short and raised me.

Hid me from the school in Albuquerque. In her shadow
my soul grew long again. I heard there were herds of wild horses
in the northern fields of the reservation.

Grandmother said her first husband gave six horses for her,
but still, the second husband had been the best.

I could not tell her but nights I dreamed those horses
were six handsome men, and finally I chose the most galloping
one, a good Apache cattleman from Three Rivers.

MY GRANDFATHER'S LAND

This quarter-mile on the river was my grandfather's.

He was born here in 1831.
There was no priest, but the people knew long prayers, then
and if a boy was born they killed a rooster, and played guitars.

Those days the cottonwoods were watchful angels.
The Mother of God walked the little canyons.

She always looked like a humble woman but her blue mantle hid
a thousand stars she could throw over you
if you stayed at the river until dark.

There was plenty of mint and horsetail and wild strawberries.

My grandfather Inocente died young, but last night I dreamed him
older than these hills.
His voice was in these slender trees we planted two years ago
when the river carried away his apple orchard.

I told him our trouble and fell asleep, naked and drunk
as faith on whiskey next to my wife, Guadalupe.

If there are no records at the courthouse. If the Mormons or the Texans
step forward with false documents, then turn to the wind
and the sun and the trees. They carry the truth. Ask for my name.

That was his advice.
When the ranchers came with their rifles I didn't break
the sixth commandment for the sake of Guadalupe and our children.

They let us take our belongings, our horses and wagon,
our milk cow and our chickens, even the eggs we gathered that morning.
Everything except the old house and the land

that had blessed us for one hundred years.

It's a sin, and I can't tell my wife but I still pray
those men swept away by flood in the canyon.

I pray their ten horses were all Our Lord and Savior Jesus Christ
who ran down the shortest road to hell,
fast and without a bridle.

LIGHTNING

I've been struck so many times no one stands near me
anymore, except my wife. When it storms,
I don't dare shelter under any tree but a juniper,
since they're charmed.

Neighbors are far off, but if they hear a loud shot,
they know it's me and most likely I'm alright.

I've been struck out riding fence. On horseback, on foot. In a barn
with the swallows watching from the rafters.

Staring at clouds flat on the bottom of a clear river.
In a hollow log with a gentle bull snake.
In the passenger seat of my Silver City nephew's new Ford.

Once I left the ranch house door ajar and a bolt rode in
without knocking and blasted my coffee cup out of my hands.
My wife brought me another cup, just as good.

I've been struck everywhere except in bed,
and the woman and I are grateful for that.

My grandpa was half-Indian. He got this land here near the Black Range
and wouldn't go back to his Oklahoma claim
because he didn't trust the government.

Grandma was Creek and she got so mad she went to live
by herself in a clapboard house a quarter-mile up the road.
She made his supper and set in on the porch every evening at seven o'clock
until she died in that there old iron-framed bed
but she never spoke to him again.

He buried her the Indian way she wanted. Wrapped in a pretty blanket,
without a box.

Since you're only the wind I'll tell you why I think
lightning's following me.

It's tired and it's lonely. It's a medicine like a hawk that's just
looking for a place to rest.
Another secret is that when a man gets struck
his heart changes to a woman's. When a woman gets struck it's just
the opposite. I've heard my wife say
she can't even tell anymore what a big and hollow
place this sky is.

MOUNTAIN LION, 1936

I was his shadow. The one Ben Lily hoped to kill
that morning he died in the poorhouse in Silver City.

I escaped, ran free from his dogs who were mourning
against the adobe wall, the iron of my blood
lost to their tongues.

I was his shadow. He first saw me in the Louisiana canebrakes
and killed my brother the black bear with a pocketknife.

That was fifty years ago. He followed that hawk bothering
his wife he called that daughter of Gomorrah's chickens,
and kept going.

He tracked me state to state across the west.
Mountain to mountain. Killed thousands of bears, hundreds
of lions. Saw my golden twin sister swaying

in the highest branch of a tall pine and shot her paw.
Drilled her heart when she was halfway
to the ground.

I was his shadow. He forgot his money paid by grateful
ranchers in banks across Texas and New Mexico.
Wrote checks on the fragments of bone
for what he wanted, maybe once a year, in December.

He slept with his dogs beneath dried leaves. They unburied what I killed,
cooked it in fire for the strength to hound me over
rocks, pine needles.

Rested only on days Lily suspected were Sundays.
Then he sat and read his Bible. Walked solemn
through pages of desert valleys, deer and blue water.

I called him The Judge.
He called me The Devil.
Because I could wreak evil in these piñon and juniper hills
and was not ashamed. He never stopped his human talking, kept it
up like a prayer. I called him Shame.

He called me Cain. On nights he slept I crept close to his face.
Studied it and almost loved him like a brother.
On his forehead there was a mark
like a smoke stain on an altar.

Mary Burritt
      Christiansen
Poetry Series

Poet Mary Burritt Christiansen's (1923–1998)
literary philanthropy expresses
a generosity of spirit that will befriend
the creative committment of poets
for years to come.

As she wished, her bequest shall be used for
the publication of significant works of poetry
from an international body of contributors
of established and newly emerging authors.

V. B. Price
SERIES EDITOR

Dianne Edwards
UNIVERSITY OF NEW MEXICO PRESS POETRY EDITOR